THE PSYCHOLOGY OF PHILOSOPHERS

THE PSYCHOLOGY OF PHILOSOPHERS

ALEXANDER HERZBERG

GYAN

Published by

GYAN

Gyan Publishing House
5, Ansari Road
Daryaganj, New Delhi-110002
Phone: 011-47034999, 9811692060
E-mail: books@gyanbooks.com

Distribution Network
gyanbooks.com
India, USA, Canada, UK, Australia

ISBN: 978-93-6780-024-9 (HB)

First Published, 1929

2nd Impression 2024

Printed at: Gyan Press, Delhi.

THE PSYCHOLOGY OF PHILOSOPHERS
Author: ALEXANDER HERZBERG

The Psychology of Philosophers

The Psychology of Philosophers

By

ALEXANDER HERZBERG

LONDON
KEGAN PAUL, TRENCH, TRUBNER & CO. LTD.
NEW YORK: HARCOURT, BRACE & COMPANY
1929

CONTENTS

CONTENTS

FOREWORD

We may ask how a person comes to develop a particular neurosis with the curious symptoms which often accompany neuroses. We may also ask what kind of person develops neuroses and what kind does not: psychoanalysis is concerned with finding the answer to both questions. In the same way we may inquire how a person comes to develop his particular theory of life and what sort of person he must be to develop one, for it does not happen to everybody. After many others had made the attempt, Müller-Freienfels answered the first question categorically and systematically by the statement that a person's outlook upon life is determined by his intellectual and emotional structure; the second question has not yet formed the subject of such general and intensive study.

The purpose of this book is to supply the deficiency and to answer the question why anyone constructs an outlook on life for himself or, to be more precise, becomes a philosopher. I have enumerated the factors which must be present in a man's mind in order that he may become a thinker, and above all a great thinker, for we are here thinking of a theory of life mainly in the philosophical sense and not in the wider sense in which the term is used by Müller-Freienfels, who makes it include both artistic outlook and religious creed. Still, having regard to the close connexion of the three fields of study, the problem of the artist and that of the man of religion must also be touched upon.

I will lay my cards on the table at once with an answer to Gretchen's question :—

" How stands it with religion in thy mind ? "

The " religion " with which we are here concerned is psycho-analysis. My attitude is one neither of disbelief nor of adoration, but is selective and critical. Apart from certain fundamental points of agreement which lie in the non-phenomenological, analytical, treatment of the pyschology of the philosophers, in the demonstration of the requisite *psychical* factors and in the attribution of high value to the impulses, I have also taken over directly certain psycho-analytical teachings, in particular those of sublimation and of the development of neuroses through the insufficient satisfaction of impulses—though with not inconsiderable changes. On the other hand, I have not accepted the theories which regard sex curiosity as underlying the general desire for knowledge, the repression of sex impulse as the origin of philosophical thought, and sexual interests as of primary importance over the other interests of life and thought. These and many other similar theories which also seemed to me untenable have been replaced by other and, I venture to hope, better ones.

ALEXANDER HERZBERG.

Berlin, January, 1926.

INTRODUCTION

PRELIMINARY HISTORICAL REMARKS

WHAT manner of man may become a philosopher is a question which engaged Plato's attention. His answer was that he must be one to whom " nature shall have given a retentive memory and made him quick at learning, lofty-minded and graceful, the friend and brother of truth, justice, fortitude and temperance."[1] To these qualities, however, something must be added to prevent him from following the allurements of riches and fame or to hold him back from politics in their present state—ill-health or an inner warning voice. But outward restraints such as condemnation to exile or the narrow life of petty States, upon which a large-minded man looks down with contempt, may take the place of these inner factors.[2]

Schopenhauer believed that the common factor of philosophic and artistic genius is the predominance of intellect over will: whilst the ordinary man consists, so to speak, of two parts of will to one of intellect, the proportions are reversed in the genius, who possesses far more intellect than is necessary to the satisfaction of his will and whose intellect succeeds at times in shaking itself free from the harness of practical interests and contemplating the world, in Schopenhauer's words, as a pure

[1] *Republic*, 487. [2] *Ibid*, 496.

eye of the spirit and a purely perceptive entity. Such contemplation he regarded as essential to true philosophic or artistic accomplishment.

Nietzsche stressed what was morbid and ineffectual in the character of past philosophers. In his mind they were sickly and ineffective people who created refuges from life for themselves, " but in order to suffer from reality one must be a bungled portion of it."[1]

For Hitschmann, a philosopher is a man in whom " a particularly strong impulse towards inquiry, diverted from the sexual field, reappears as a philosophic impulse to acquire knowledge, reinforcing intellectual activities with a sense of pleasure."[2] In order, however, that a man shall continue to devote himself to philosophic problems he must have been disillusioned by life and this disillusionment is in turn rooted in a pathological predisposition.

These views contain a highly valuable contribution to the problem of the philosophers, mixed however with much that is untenable. It is the purpose of this book to sift out what is untenable and to retain what is valuable, proving it empirically and supplementing it.

[1] *Works*, XVI, p. 142.

[2] p. 163.

CHAPTER I

WHAT PHILOSOPHY WAS

WHAT is philosophy? This is a question on which those who should be best informed, *i.e.*, the philosophers of all times, are notoriously disagreed. Plato understood it to be the perception of ideas, that is to say, of the independent and essential being of things, whereas Aristotle identified it with knowledge as a whole. For the Stoics, it was love of wisdom and virtue, for the Epicureans, wisely directed effort towards happiness. Descartes saw in philosophy the complete knowledge of all things which man can know—a knowledge derived from first causes. Schopenhauer says in effect much the same thing: it is the function of philosophy to restate the essentials of the world in terms of concepts; and so does Wundt to whom philosophy represents knowledge as a whole and has the duty of combining the truths brought to light by the separate branches of science into a system devoid of contradictions. Lipps gives a more restrictive definition: philosophy is the science of spiritual things; and Riehl a narrower one still, for he regards theoretical philosophy solely as the science of perception, practical philosophy supplementing it as the art of guiding the spirit. Windelband gives a quite different definition —that of the science of values.

The causes of these differences of opinion are to be sought partly in the fact that every philosopher is inclined to regard his own sphere of investigation and what is connected with it as the whole field of philosophy, and consequently to overlook efforts tending in other directions, and partly in the changes which have actually come about in the nature of philosophy at different epochs, for, like all living things—especially intellectual ones—it has undergone a process of evolution during the ages.

We see the first phase of this process in the *Upanishads*, in the elegies of Xenophanes with their religious tone, and in Plato's *Phaedo*, *Phaedrus*, and *Timaeus*. It is true that these works are concerned with the essence of things or with the recognition of things from their causes; we may also find in them the effort to attain to wisdom and virtue and, not least, the art of guiding the spirit. But they contain more, and not one of the definitions which we have mentioned fully covers the content of this philosophy, because none does justice to the artistic value and the religious fire with which they are instinct and which combine with the perceptual and practical components to form an indivisible whole.

How then are we to regard works of this kind?

It is customary to divide the spiritual life of all peoples and ages into three main parts which, in spite of common ground at numerous points, are capable of fairly sharp distinction. These are religion, art and science. It is generally not difficult to say of any given work to which of the three groups it belongs: thus we can classify the teachings of Mohammed, the poems of Homer, or the Copernican planetary system without difficulty.

But how are we to classify the works which we have just mentioned—the *Upanishads* or Plato's *Phaedo* or such later works as the teachings of Plotinus, the *Confessions* of St Augustine or Schopenhauer's doctrine of deliverance?

If we are unable to give a direct and, as it were, an intuitive answer to the question whether these works are concerned with religion, art, or science, with none of them, or with all three, it only remains for us to make clear what we understand by religion, art and science and then to establish whether the characteristics of one or more of these groups may be found in the works concerned.

What then is religion? In spite of all differences of conviction and rite, its common content is in every case man's share in the life of a superhuman being—whether known as God, or the World-soul, or the All-embracing Being—a life shared in the way that the lives of father and child are shared and thus based on love and respect, or in some cases conceived as a merging of man with this higher power.

The feeling of such a community of life and the effort to realize it or to render it more efficacious runs through all the philosophic works which we have mentioned, whether in the more primitive form of the *Confessions* of St Augustine and Plato's *Phaedo* or in the higher form of the teachings of Plotinus, the *Upanishads*, or Schopenhauer's doctrine of deliverance, and to this extent the content of these works must be called religion.

But if we are to define as a work of art a thing which depicts aspects of reality that are important to our emotional life, then we must regard the *Upanishads*, *Phaedo*, the *Confessions* of St Augustine, and Schopenhauer's philosophy of deliverance as works of art and powerful ones.

And finally, if science is to be found where definitions, problems, perceptions and proofs are systematically developed, we are compelled to admit that all the above-mentioned works have scientific aspects, though in part of a primitive kind. They ask questions as to the relation of the individual to the world as a whole, as to the nature and destiny of the soul, whence evil comes into the world or how the world may be delivered from suffering—problems enough. Answers are given to these questions, that is to say, items of knowledge are proffered. Nor is faith alone required in exchange, for proofs are adduced. Thus we see science at work even though co-ordination and clear definition are only in their beginnings.

If then we can classify a number of philosophic creations with equal justice under the headings of religion, art, or science, if we find that their scientific aspects are of a primitive kind, and if, finally, we observe that such works were at first relatively numerous and later increasingly rare, we are forced to the conclusion that this marks an early stage in the evolution of the human spirit, one in which religion, poetry and science, like rudimentary organs lying undeveloped side by side in a spiritual embryo, are not yet differentiated.

In this stage of development, philosophy is therefore *a still undifferentiated whole comprising religion, poetry and science.*

From this point the poetic aspect falls into the background and further evolution proceeds in two directions. The one, determined by the increasingly unhampered development of the perceptual impulse, tends towards knowledge and is theoretical philosophy; whilst the other, more closely allied to religious effort, seeking to lay down life-ideals and standards of conduct and thus tending towards a rule of life, is practical philosophy. The two tendencies are by no means strictly separated from one another, for theories are constantly and intentionally introduced as a basis for life-ideals and in their turn life-ideals often unconsciously determine the theories. But the division is into representative types and the emphasis falls on the one tendency or on the other.

What then is theoretical philosophy? Examples of what is given this name are supplied by some of Plato's dialogues, *e.g.*, the *Theaetetus*, and by numerous works of Aristotle, *e.g.*, those on logic, physics, zoology, the soul, the art of poetry and the State. We find it in Descartes' *Meditations*, in Locke's *Essay*, in Leibniz's *Monadology*, in Kant's *Critique of Pure Reason*, in the first three books of Schopenhauer's main work, in Spencer's *System* and in Mach's *Analysis of Sensations*. The common measure, however, of all these works—enormously though they differ from one another in the problems they raise and the answers they provide—is that they do raise problems at all, that they seek and find solutions for them and bring forward evidence in favour of these solutions. Moreover, all this is done with the help of clearly formulated and co-ordinated notions and, in a word, shews all the signs which we have mentioned as characteristic of science.

Thus, theoretical philosophy is science.

This answer leads however at once to a fresh question: if philosophy is science, how does it differ from mathematics, physics, history—in short, from other sciences?

There seem to be only two possible answers: sciences can differ in their methods of work, as mathematics differs from the empirical sciences, or they can differ in subject, as zoology differs from botany.

That philosophy differs from the other sciences in its method is an assumption the germ of which was already present in the Platonic scheme of ideas and in the cognate attempts made by Plotinus, Eckhard and other mystics to attain to knowledge through ecstasy. Spinoza, too, to whom nothing neo-Platonic was unknown, recognized the special path to knowledge which intuition provides. This form of perception was of set purpose given by Schelling the place of honour under the name of "intellectual perception" as the one peculiar to philosophy and embodying the method which distinguishes it from the other sciences; and Hegel, whilst substituting dialectics for intuition, also saw a characteristic of philosophy in its special method. With the collapse of speculative philosophy this belief in a methodological distinction between philosophy and the other sciences has been proved invalid: philosophy gained nothing from having a special method and consequently returned to the method of the other sciences, *i.e.*, the application of thought to experience.

If, then, philosophy has no special method, perhaps it can be distinguished from the other sciences by the special subject of which it treats? But what special subject can be attributed to a science which concerns itself with asking questions as much about the essence and nature of judgments as about the various forms of public life, deals with problems both of physics and of æsthetics, and inquires into the essence of the soul no less than into the animal anatomy? Such a science has no special subject, it is the science of everything, universal science, and differs from the other sciences as the whole differs from the part—or rather, it would so differ if there were other sciences. But at a certain stage of development there are no other sciences as yet and at this stage—as represented, approximately, by Aristotle—*philosophy is the primitive form of science, the germ-cell, in which the rudiments of all sciences lie undifferentiated side by side.*

We must thus distinguish two phases through which philosophy has passed—that of the undifferentiated, religious-poetic-scientific creations and that of philosophy as an undifferentiated universal science closely associated with practical philosophy in the form of a rule of life. The two phases are not sharply separated in point of time: they coincided for a long period, so that originally, in Indian and Greek antiquity and up to the time of Plato, the former predominated; the second drew level with Aristotle and predominated from the beginning of the seventeenth century—subject, however, to numerous set-backs, notably those due to Schelling and Schopenhauer.

CHAPTER II

WHAT PHILOSOPHY IS

UNDER the pressure of practical requirements, the evolutionary process which led to the division of the earliest works of the spirit into religion, poetry and science continued to exert itself in primitive science, which thus showed a steady tendency to divide into independent branches—firstly mathematics, then astronomy and physics, later chemistry, then biology, and finally psychology and sociology.

Let us suppose that this process of differentiation, which has to-day gone as far as psychology, had come to an end and that logic, the theory of knowledge, ethics and æsthetics had become completely independent sciences; what would then remain of philosophy?

One obvious answer, which in point of fact represents the opinion of positivist investigators such as Ostwald, is—nothing. Philosophy would be a historical memory, an abandoned standpoint, an empty shell, like those of the unicellular organisms which form daughter-cells and, after the latter's growth and escape, remain behind as abandoned husks.

The process is, however, not yet completed; psychology is still fighting for independence, and logic, the theory of knowledge, ethics and æsthetics are only beginning their battles. That is why, in Ostwald's view, philosophy still exists to-day. It is a vestigiary phenomenon, made up of the above-mentioned, not yet independent, sciences, and it is, so to speak, no longer anything more than a stopgap.

This attitude is strongly opposed from various points of view. Its opponents are at one in denying the ephemeral character of philosophy; for all of them it is something permanent, something that remains even after the separate branches of science have attained independence, but to each it means something different.

An influential section[1] among them considers that philosophy can be justified as a separate science by its special subject and that this subject is to be found in the separate branches themselves. The latter are, it is contended, sciences concerned with reality, whereas philosophy is the science of the sciences, the knowledge of knowledge, which, as such, must show the forms and methods inherent in the scientific adduction of proof and demonstrate the basic ideas common to the separate sciences, investigate their relations with one another and test the value of their claims.

Others believe that the study of knowledge is only a part of philosophy but that philosophy has a wider field —the widest possible, in fact—namely, the whole range of physical and psychical reality, including such spiritual values as religion, law, morality, art and science.[2] In spite of all its differentiation into separate branches, they regard it as remaining what it has always been since it

[1] Including, in particular, Kuno Fischer and A. Riehl.

[2] Among the many adherents of this view, W. Wundt and F. Paulsen may be mentioned.

came to be a science at all, namely, the sum of all sciences—universal science. The justification for such a universal science, is, in their opinion, the fact that the respective fields of the separate sciences are not divided off from one another but are connected by close relationships and transitions as parts of a comprehensive and real whole.

There is truth, as we shall see later, in both of these standpoints, but it is mixed with error. The key to our recognition of this and also to a third standpoint is furnished by the fact that in nearly all spheres of knowledge a distinction is made between interesting problems and results and such as leave the philosopher indifferent. The facts that silver is the best conductor of electricity, that gold is soluble in *aqua-regia*, that tortoises have horned plates instead of teeth, and that a piece of poetry which has been learned by heart will be forgotten quickly at first and more slowly afterwards are very interesting and important truths for the physicist, the chemist, the zoologist and the psychologist, but to the philosopher they are irrelevant. On the other hand, such questions as what light is, whether all bodies are composed of one or more ultimate substances, whether species are constant or subject to change, or how physical and cerebral processes are interconnected are problems which have always aroused the greatest interest, not only of the scientist in the branch directly concerned, but also of the philosopher.

And the distinction between what is philosophically interesting and what is philosophically irrelevant applies just as much to whole branches of science as to facts arising within the limits of each branch. Thus, commercial law and mineralogy are of comparatively little philosophical interest, whilst logic and the theory of knowledge are regarded as of eminent philosophical importance.

If we now turn to the individual problems and the branches of science which we have just cited as being philosophically interesting and examine them in the light of what they—as distinct from those classed as philosophically irrelevant—have in common, we find that they raise problems of a far-reaching character and questions of wide, indeed, the widest, import. Such are the physical question as to the nature of light, the chemical question as to the ultimate composition of matter or the zoological question as to the evolution of species, numerous questions raised by logic, and all those raised by the theory of knowledge. In addition, there are certain problems, such as the meaning of life, which have always been regarded as essentially philosophic ones, for they do not fall within the scope of any one science and can only be solved by the co-operation of several—in the case at issue, astronomy, physics, biology, psychology and sociology.

Philosophy, however, is the sum of all things which are philosophically interesting or philosophically relevant. Thus it can be neither the mere doctrine of knowledge nor a system of all sciences but must be the science of the most general problems in all fields. Its function is to bring together the answers to these problems, that is to say, the most general results of all sciences, into a scheme of life as a whole.

Though it has often been observed that, if philosophy

is to be restricted to wide and universal problems, the boundaries separating it from the individual sciences cannot be otherwise than ill-defined, this fact is seldom raised as an objection against the opinion in question, for the boundaries between physics and chemistry, physics and the theory of knowledge, zoology and botany, physiology and psychology are equally ill-defined.

It is easy to see that this conception of philosophy as a science of the most general problems affords a remarkable combination of the two conceptions to which reference has already been made. The doctrine of knowledge would be allotted to philosophy because it deals with the most general problems, but philosophy would remain the synthesis of all sciences, not, as the second conception would hold, in their smallest details, but only as a sort of quintessence of all sciences and of their wider results.

The view outlined above, that philosophy must disappear as the result of the splitting up of general science into special sciences, is thus refuted ; philosophy must be allotted a special field, comprising the most general problems of all other fields, and a special task, namely, the solution of these problems and the synthesis of the solutions into a general scheme of things. We will deal later with the contention that philosophy's claim upon these problems involves their inclusion in, rather than their exclusion from, the sphere of the separate sciences.[1]

We now come to another question : the problems of interest to philosophy are of a general character and of wide scope ; have they no further characteristics by

[1] See p. 17.

means of which they may be distinguished from those subjects which are solely of interest to the special branches of science? Let us compare such questions as that regarding the tortoise's masticatory apparatus or the rate of forgetting with the question of the origin of species or the relations between body and soul. The latter are the more general, it is true, but they are also not so purely academic; they are more instinct with life and touch us more directly. This is the case with very many problems, including even some of a more special nature which always were, and still are, accounted philosophic.

Freedom of the will and immortality appeal to us in a different way from the mechanism of reflexes or even the conservation of energy; they are closer to life, they arouse more discussion, we feel that they touch upon *our* vital interests. And again, there are whole branches of science in which this peculiar closeness to life and this direct effect upon our emotions are present in an especially high degree. Such are psychology and ethics, and here again we see with the greatest clarity that these sciences have always been, and still are, regarded as part of philosophy.

We may make due allowance for these facts by extending our former definition of philosophy thus: *philosophy is the science of the widest problems in all fields and of those problems which affect mankind most closely.* Its task is to find answers to them and to combine them into a coherent scheme of life.

And finally, a word about practical philosophy. What *was* it? Socrates shows it to us and so do Plato, the Stoics and the Epicureans, Plotinus and St Augustine—

as the scientifically supported assertion and propagation of life-ideals together with an indication of the path which makes them accessible, and lastly the practice itself, *i.e.*, life, in which they can be realized. What is it now? The same thing, for Spinoza as a practical philosopher has done no more—nor has Schopenhauer, Nietzsche, or Müller-Lyer.

Let us summarize the result of our inquiry into the nature of philosophy:—

1. Philosophy was originally an infantile stage in the life of the human spirit—the undifferentiated germ-cell of religion, poetry and science;

2. Philosophy then became an infantile stage of science—the undifferentiated germ-cell of all sciences;

3. Philosophy is to-day the science which combines into a general scheme of things the most general truths and those truths which chiefly affect the human emotions;

4. Practical philosophy is the assertion, the establishment, the propagation, and the practice of life-ideals.

CHAPTER III

WHY PHILOSOPHY IS REGARDED AS A HOMOGENEOUS SCIENCE

ZOOLOGY is the science of animals, a group of units which by reason of resemblance, transition stages and development out of one another, show a certain homogeneity. The fact that there exists an independent science known as zoology is due to this homogeneity of its subject.

Medicine treats of physical, chemical, zoological, botanical, anatomical, physiological, psychological and other themes; the motive, however, for their selection and the tie which unites them are the prevention and cure of illness, *i.e.*, a single purpose.

Thus a homogeneous subject of study—as in zoology, botany, astronomy, physics or chemistry—or a single purpose—as in medicine, education or politics—furnishes the motive underlying the selection and synthesis by means of which a given science becomes homogeneous and different from others.

Philosophy is the science of the widest problems and of those which most closely affect mankind. Is not this a remarkable combination? From quite different fields of study one set of problems and results is collected which have nothing more to do with one another than the fact that they are all of a general nature; another set is added having a common characteristic which is, objectively speaking, still more indifferent—that of a strong appeal to the emotions—and these two sets are then to be combined to constitute philosophy. How is this to come about? Where is the reason for the selection, where the motive for the synthesis? It is not to be found in singleness of subject, for the subjects belong to the most varied fields. There remains singleness of purpose. And indeed, in the case of theoretical philosophy, with which for the time being we are alone concerned, a common purpose of this kind has always been assumed—that of the satisfaction of the desire for knowledge, of the impulse to theorize. Pythagoras, Cicero tells us, gave this as his own purpose and, in the same way, Plato and Aristotle regard astonishment and Descartes regards doubt—both of which are emotions arising out of the lack of intellectual satisfaction—as sources of philosophy.

Though the desire for knowledge is directed towards knowing, it does not accept all forms of knowledge indifferently; on the contrary, a perception will afford the greater satisfaction in proportion as it is more comprehensive and allows more specific knowledge to be deduced from it, thus permitting the general body of ascertained truth to be drawn more closely together. Hence it is comprehensible that philosophy treats essentially of general problems, for they are the ones which arouse the greatest intellectual interest and it is their solution that creates the greatest satisfaction.

Philosophy is therefore a science so long as it is pursued from purely theoretical interest or, to express the same idea in different words, a science having for its purpose the satisfaction of the impulse to construct theories.

But cannot mathematics, astronomy, chemistry or biology also be pursued from purely theoretical interest? Though, undeniably, practical reasons were strongly represented at the inception and during the development of these and most of the other special sciences, we need only think of research into the problems of squaring the circle, the composition of the stars, the periodical system of the elements or the causes of organic development in order to answer this question in the affirmative. Then is a person engaged in these sciences from theoretical interest engaged in philosophy? Yes, in so far as he has the more general problems in mind and concerns only himself with the particular for the sake of the general.[1] Newton is justified in calling his work *Natural Philosophy* and Lamarck in calling his *Zoological Philosophy*, because these works aim at general results and only treat of special questions as a means to the end.[2]

What then is the situation of the inveterate specialist who, not troubling about the general value of knowledge and still less about any practical end, devotes himself out of purely theoretical interest to calculating the path of comets or to describing varieties of earth-worms? Is he also engaged in philosophy? The question shows us that the definition of philosophy as a science in so far as it is pursued from purely theoretical interest is inadequate, because too loose, for it includes a form of

[1] See p. 12.

[2] Cf. Paulsen, *Einleitung in die Philosophie* (p. 37). The works quoted will be mentioned in the footnotes by the name of the author alone. Titles, edition and year of publication will be found in the bibliography at the end of the book. Where several works by one writer are mentioned the title of the work concerned is given in an abbreviated form.

activity which has never been accounted philosophy but always regarded as directly opposed to it.

Philosophy is, however, not only the science of the most general problems but also of those which especially arouse the human emotions. Cannot this latter definition of the subject of philosophy be called upon to complete our understanding of its purpose ?

Why has the question of immortality occupied philosophers so much ? Schopenhauer gives us the answer when he says that Death is the genius that inspires philosophy ; certainly death inspired the question of immortality, for behind this question and its answers—which are after all for the most part more or less positive—the life-impulse, the primitive, instinctive fear of death is present. And not it alone ; reward or punishment await the soul in the life beyond or in some later incarnation ; this proves that the instinct for requital—both the thirst for revenge and the wish to be rewarded for one's own virtues or sacrifices—determines the interest in this problem.

And again : whence comes the lively interest shown by philosophers, or—since in this matter nearly everybody is a philosopher—by men in general, in God ? Here again the above-mentioned impulses play a part, for God is the chief guarantor of immortality and of requital.

In the main, however, it is the need for support—arising out of the terrible feeling of helplessness in the face of the dangers of life, its emergencies and anxieties—that explains the interest taken in this problem and in its solutions, which are, again, for the most part positive.

Again, why does the problem of free will excite people's

minds so much? Because here too a mighty impulse is concerned: humanity's urge towards freedom, mistaking causality for compulsion, revolts against the inferences to be drawn from the study of nature.

And finally, although the most general problems have always aroused such glowing interest amongst philosophers, it has by no means always, or even often, been a purely theoretical one. The answer to the question as to the nature of the world, for instance, must to a considerable extent determine the solution of those problems—such as immortality or freedom—which are of a more special kind but thereby affect us the more closely. Indeed, such emotional interests may even attach to problems of knowledge: Plato, for example, combines the problem of the origin of ideas with that of the pre-existence and immortality of the soul and Kant the problem of the *a priori* validity of synthetic judgments with that of the justification for the belief in God, freedom and immortality.

We may sum up by saying that the interest felt in numerous and important philosophical problems is not a purely theoretical one but is based on powerful impulses which press for gratification; in a word, it springs not from the intellect but from the will, the emotions. "All great things," says Riehl, "—and philosophy is one of them—come from the heart and from great passion."[1]

If, then, we have said above that the motive underlying selection, according to which philosophy determines what falls within its scope, is theoretical interest, we must

[1] A. Riehl, *Nietzsche*, p. 11.

now add that this motive is a double one, compounded of theoretical and of emotional interest as opposed to the practical interest which determines the choice of subject in medicine, politics or education. A double standpoint and yet a single one, for theoretical and emotional interest combine to form what is called philosophic interest. Why they do so can in part be explained and has indeed already been indicated. The emotional interest which attaches directly only to certain more special problems passes over to general ones because their solution determines that of the special ones and coincides with theoretical interest. Furthermore, philosophic questions affecting the emotions are still general enough to arouse theoretical interest. The other, deeper, reason for this merging of interests will be seen later.[1]

In any case the philosophic interest thus composed of heterogeneous parts, which nevertheless form subjectively a solid common front, motivates the selection and the synthesis of the subjects which go to make philosophy.

Philosophy also differs from other sciences, whether they are pursued from practical or from theoretical interest, through the predominance of its specific trend of interest, a result of the combination of theoretical and emotional interest: philosophy is science so long as it is pursued from this unique interest formed out of a theoretical and an emotional need.

Its satisfaction is the single purpose of philosophy, the bond which holds its components together in spite of their tendency to disintegrate.

[1] See p. 121.

To sum up: what makes philosophy a homogeneous science is its single purpose—the satisfaction of the philosophic need. This need, which subjectively appears to be a simple one, is compounded of theoretical and of emotional interest.

CHAPTER IV

THE NATURE AND ORIGIN OF PHILOSOPHIC INTEREST

For those who, like ourselves, are concerned with the psychology of philosophy, philosophic interest is of especial importance as representing the psychological factor, or rather complex of factors, underlying both receptive and productive philosophic thought—reason enough for us to examine it more closely.

What, first of all, is an interest? A child is greatly interested in food and drink; what does this mean? It means that the child endeavours to attain these things when he lacks them and to retain them when he is in danger of losing them. Again, it gives him pleasure to concern himself with them—both with food and drink themselves and with occupations directly connected with them, such as shopping and preparing food. Thirdly, food and drink, together with objects and pursuits connected with them, arouse his particular attention.

Or let us take the case of a Don Juan. His interests are predominantly erotic, *i.e.*, he is chiefly concerned with women, this concern gives him pleasure, and everything connected with it arouses and holds his interest in the highest degree.

The man who is interested in mathematics makes every effort to acquire mathematical knowledge which leaves others indifferent; working at mathematics, which is misery to his fellows, is a pleasure to him; the shapes of solids, geometrical forms and the relationships of numbers, which other people do not notice, arouse his attention.

Whether the subject of interest is clothes or furniture, one's profession or one's travels, the theatre or music, literature, politics, or science, it will always show itself in the three symptoms—assiduity, pleasure in the occupation, and heightened sensibility and attentiveness to everything connected with it.

The psychological explanation of all three groups of phenomena is as follows: there exists a complex of residues of previous perceptions, whether regarding food or sport or postage stamps; this complex is associated with a complex of predispositions to the corresponding actions, eating, athletic exercise and collecting, and is easily excited by certain peripheral stimuli or the corresponding organic sensations—such, for instance, as hunger or sexual desire—or by observing or imagining the object of the impulse. The excitement is conveyed to the motor dispositive complexes and thereby impels to action, the factor of endeavour being thus produced. The unimpeded flow of excitement stimuli to the motor region is fraught with pleasure—hence the feeling of satisfaction in the occupation. Finally, the ready excitability of the perceptual dispositive complexes explains the attitude of attentiveness, for we quickly become attentive to impressions for which easily stimulated dispositive complexes are available.

If it is desired to substitute a single phrase for this

rather complicated description we may say that interests are predispositions to endeavour, or latent endeavours.

Whence does interest come? In the case of many interests the answer is easily found: the interest in food and drink naturally arises out of the corresponding feelings of hunger or thirst; if as the result of a surfeit of food or illness these impulses cease either temporarily or permanently to make themselves felt, the interest also disappears, however great it may have been before. We have said above that the dispositive complexes which deal with the perceptions regarding food and drink are stimulated by the organic sensations of hunger and thirst. Erotic interests arise in the same way out of the sexual impulse, and interest in children out of the impulse to care for offspring. By the side of these three great impulses, the impulse, associated with every form of dislike, to avoid objects of dislike, plays an important part. Even among monkeys, cold produces an interest in rugs; a man with neuralgia will display an interest in anodynes and the unhappily married begin to take an interest in the divorce columns. In the same way as every dislike, every pleasure is accompanied by an impulse which may become a source of interests, namely, the impulse to repeat the experience. Thus some people are interested in sweets or in fireworks—and some in alcohol or morphia. In the last resort, of course, every interest may be traced back to the impulse to repeat a pleasure. Where, however, it is not a case of pleasurable sensation directly connected with the sense-impressions, *e.g.*, tastes or colours, we must inquire further into the origin of the sensation of pleasure—as in the case of the interest in postage stamps, novels, or mathematics—though by so doing we are merely setting the problem of the origin of the interest a stage back.

If we take up this problem again and inquire, for example, into the origin of the interest in clothes, we find naturally that the primary impulse concerned is that of seeking refuge from cold. In addition, the sense of shame plays a part; the desire, however, is not merely to be dressed, but to be well dressed, and therefore vanity, that is to say in the final analysis sexual impulse-components, is also represented. From this it is clear that an interest may proceed from the combination of several impulses. Careful observation will show that most interests are constituted in this way: thus, professional interest is frequently based not only on the impulse for gain—which is in itself a compound one—but, in the case of the research worker, in part on the impulse to acquire knowledge, and in the soldier, partly on the combative instincts.

Finally, there are many interests which steadfastly resist the attempt to analyse them. We are still unable to say why one person is interested in mathematics or astronomy whilst another is interested in music or painting. If the same were the case with the philosophic interests, our inquiry would be already at an end and its result could be expressed in the words: philosophy has its origin in a specific interest, known as the philosophic interest, which is found in numerous human beings but we do not know why.

I hope, however, that in this case it will be possible to say why.

But first of all—what is philosophic interest ? That we have already said : it is interest in the more general problems and truths of all kinds and in those problems which especially arouse the human emotions.

Then—whence does it come ? Does it arise, like interest in dress or professional interest, out of a number of impulses and, if so, which ? Here, too, the answer has already been given ; philosophic interest is composed, as we have seen, of theoretical and of emotional interests ; the first component is therefore theoretical interest, *i.e.*, interest in knowledge *per se*, apart from any practical utility—intellectual need or the impulse to acquire knowledge.

Doubt might be cast upon the existence of such an impulse and an attempt made to advance other impulses, *e.g.*, the extraction of practical utility from the knowledge, the obtaining of other personal advantages, vanity, or sexual interest—in explanation of its outward manifestations. Two facts, however, speak eloquently for the existence of a special impulse to acquire knowledge : the child's " why ? " and the existence of such purely theoretical sciences as logic. It is true that there are people who engage in these things in order to obtain professional advantages, or from vanity, but neither such advantages nor the satisfaction of vanity could be attained were there not a public interested in these studies and drawn towards them by the desire for knowledge alone.

We have said that emotional interest is the interest in certain questions which touch men closely, such as immortality, free will, and the existence of God. These interests are derived, as we have seen, from the fear of death, the longing for requital, the urge for freedom and the impulse to seek support and protection—that is to say, from a series of the most elementary and powerful impulses of mankind. Proof that it is really these impulses which raise the old questions ever anew is to be found in the fact that the latter are answered as often as the predominant impulses command and—even to-day in spite of all probability and of all science—in the way which they dictate.

This explanation as to nature and origin would be a complete answer to everything that could reasonably be asked about philosophic interest did not the answer itself embody a fresh and much more difficult question—that peculiarly difficult question which the psychology of philosophy raises. If we take into consideration the fact that the impulses to which we have just referred as the sources of emotional interest are among the most general and most powerful mainsprings of human *action*, the question arises why they should become in some men the mainsprings of *thought* and, converging with the impulse for knowledge, should be welded with it into philosophic interest.

Before we approach this problem we must, however, attempt to obtain a clear vision of the whole scope of its astonishing content.

CHAPTER V

CHARACTERISTICS OF PHILOSOPHIC THOUGHT

Philosophic interest, born of the union of powerful life-impulses with the desire for knowledge, urges to philosophic activity. What then is this activity?

Philosophy was the whole existence of such thinkers as Socrates, Diogenes, Zeno and Spinoza; it permeated their whole lives and determined their every action, and this is indeed the demand which practical philosophy makes and the prerequisite of its full development.

We shall have occasion to speak later of this practical philosophy, this philosophical life; the immediate question is, what is the field of activity of the theoretical philosopher? Theoretical philosophy is science; the activity of the scientist is thought; where he acts—as in experimental work and to a certain extent also in observation—his action is subordinated to the aims of thought. Philosophy, however, has for the most part avoided even the small amount of action which experiment and observation bring into the mental labour of science. The rationalists avoided it on principle, but, even apart from them, experimental philosophers like Fechner and Wundt are rare exceptions and, so far as observation is concerned, the philosophers have mainly occupied themselves with the observation of human actions and of their own behaviour—that is to say, with such forms of observation as require the least possible action. The pursuit of philosophy thus always represented a particularly pure form of thought; *i.e.*, unconnected with action.

This thought is characterized by psychological peculiarities not shared by the thought of everyday life or by that found in art, religion, or the specialized sciences.

We may first of all consider one of these peculiarities which makes it possible to mark off philosophic thought, in common with the thought found in all science, from all other kinds of thought—namely its scientific character. Philosophy is science, and therefore the thought which leads to it and in which it operates must be scientific. Philosophy is pursued from intellectual need, but only scientific thought can truly and permanently satisfy this need.

And what is scientific thought? Scientific thought deals with problems, not just as they happen to occur or as the needs of the day may dictate, but as they arise from the order of things *per se;* it arranges its results not in practical but in theoretical and objective order; it is systematic.[1] It does not even accept as correct everything which custom or apparent acceptability recommend but only those things which will pass severe tests in practice; it is critical. The two characteristics together give thought its scientific character and only such thought as embodies them both can to-day lay claim to be called philosophic, as distinct from everyday, religious or artistic thought.

[1] Cf. Kant, *Prolegomena*, § 23.

A further characteristic requires for its comprehension some consideration of the function of thought in life.

A dog wants to open a door for the first time.[1] He has observed that human beings do something to the handle, so he stands on his hind legs and paws it, pulling, pushing and striking; in a word, he tries all possible movements until he hits upon the combination which leads to the door's opening.

A boy sees behind a fence a flower which he would like to have. His first thought, to put his arm through, is at once rejected; the flower is too far away. He then thinks of climbing over the fence; no, the barbed wire would hurt him. He then remembers that fish are caught with hooks; why not flowers? He will bend a piece of wire and use it to take hold of the flower, break it off and pull it towards him. The idea seems a good one; he puts it into execution and attains his object.

The dog tries movements, the human being ideas; the dog learns by actual failure which movements are the wrong ones, whilst the human being is warned by the conception of failure connected, as the result of past experience, with that of an action. In the case of the dog, the right movement is recognized by success alone whereas the human being often pictures it in his thoughts beforehand and success is only a confirmation that he was right. This economically immensely important capacity of trying out thoughts, of rejecting impracticable ones and selecting the practicable is what

[1] German doors are opened by pushing a handle downwards.—*Trs.*

is called intelligence;[1] its function is invention, *i.e.*, the discovery of means whereby a definite end may be attained. We may call this form of thought mediative or means-finding thought.

Thought has, however, another function. "Do you want another pear?" the mother asks; the child pictures to itself the pear and the action of biting it, finds that the idea is associated not with pleasure but with repugnance, and says "no." "Now, shall I go for a walk or lie down?" I ask myself after a meal; the thought of going for a walk makes me feel tired, whereas the idea of lying down is fraught with pleasure, so I decide to lie down.

I am thus testing my reaction to the idea of various actions with the object of choosing between them. This capacity, which is at the same time one of high economic value because it saves the necessity of trying out the actions themselves, we will call determinative thought.[2]

The process of decision does not always follow such a simple course. The feeling of fatigue which is associated with the thought of going for a walk will not necessarily prevent me from going; a further idea may present itself, *e.g.*, that it is healthy to take exercise and that I should feel uncomfortable if I failed to do so; this idea, together with its associated suggestions of pleasure and displeasure, then plays a part in the conflict of motives and may perhaps lead me to go for a walk after all.

[1] Cf. Bühler, p. 148.

[2] Cf. Kant, *Versuch über die Krankheiten des Kopfes* (VIII, p. 71): "The intellect is only concerned here with estimating the whole extent of the general satisfaction of all tendencies arising out of the end in mind and with finding the means to it."

Whether it does this by strengthening the inclination to walk or by opposing that to lie down cannot be determined; if the question is, however, whether a given person shall, let us say, commit a theft or not—*i.e.*, whether he shall do or refrain from doing something—certain notions, such as that of punishment, may be recognized as purely dissuasive, whilst others, such as that of the advantage to be derived from the theft, are purely persuasive. But these functions, which may be called dissuasive and persuasive thought, remain forms of determinative thought; they answer the question: "What shall I do?" whilst mediative thought answers the question: "How shall I do it?"

Mediative and determinative thought have this in common, that they are not ends in themselves but are a preparation for action; we can therefore class them together as preparatory thought. Preparatory thought has its analogy in those actions which serve solely to render possible or prepare for other actions and they differ, therefore, from actions like eating and drinking, the sex activities, and games of all kinds, which are pursued for their own sake and in direct gratification of impulses.

It might appear that preparatory thought was the same thing as what is called practical thought, but such is not the case; when, for example, a mathematician casts about him for a method of giving expression to a complicated set of data, the search for these means—mediative thought—serves a theoretical purpose, *i.e.*, not to prepare for action but for further thought; it still remains preparatory thought and is not an end in itself.

Thus there exists mediative and preparatory thought not only in the practical but also in the theoretical field.

But we find in the latter field itself that not all thought is preparatory. Where ultimate problems are concerned—*i.e.*, those for the sake of which others are treated—thought is an end in itself and in the direct satisfaction of the desire for knowledge which it affords. In the same way, we experience in dreams, in waking fancies and in artistic and religious thought varieties of this mental activity, which do not serve as a preparation for action or for a further process of thought, serving, indeed, no purpose outside themselves and fulfilling themselves—as the direct emanations of impulses, strivings, wishes, or fears—exactly like such activities as play or love-making, which are also ends in themselves.[1] This form of thought may be regarded as self-contained in comparison with preparatory thought; those who believe that a scientific conception can only be preserved if it has a foreign label may call it autarchic thought, from the Stoic word "autarchy."

Let us now revert to philosophy. What is the place of philosophic thought? Does it serve to prepare for actions or processes of thought, or is it an end in itself? We will disregard practical philosophy in this connexion; but even in theoretical philosophy there is, naturally, much preparatory thought, as there is elsewhere in science, *i.e.*, everywhere where problems are treated solely as a means to the solution of other problems. In the case of

[1] The word "ends" is to be understood here in the psychological sense of purpose, not in the biological sense of utility. Biologically, actions of this kind may have an "end" outside themselves, *e.g.*, physical fitness or the begetting of offspring respectively.

these others, however, and specially in the case of the widest, the ultimate ones, which are the philosophical problems *par excellence*, the thought which is brought to bear upon them is a direct emanation of the impulse for knowledge or of the other impulses to which we have referred; it is not a means to the attainment of any practical or theoretical end outside itself; it is not means-seeking or means-finding, for in its own nature and in its results, which are, however, again only experienced as thought-images, powerful needs seek expression, urgent impulses find satisfaction, and fears and anxieties are pacified. Philosophizing, then, is autarchic thought if and in so far as it arises from the desire for acquiring knowledge or is a means whereby other impulses are set in action.

If the objection be raised that we do not think for thought's sake but for the sake of the knowledge which it is hoped to acquire by thinking, and that thought is thus only a means and never an end, we may reply that the point has been overlooked that these results can, again, only be recognized as thoughts and that it is also incorrect to say that we think only with a view to results—just as incorrect as to say that we act only with a view to results. Many actions, like eating and drinking, are performed without any definite purpose in mind and many others—*e.g.*, sport and social intercourse—not *entirely* with a definite purpose but rather in direct gratification of an impulse. Thus philosophic thought is also developed *directly* out of its impulse components; the notions of a divine protector and of immortality arise *directly* in a tortured mind fighting against the afflictions of life and the fear of death, and the question as to the meaning of life is the *direct* offshoot of the same impulses.

Philosophizing is scientific thought, we have said; we may add that it is self-sufficing thought. If the first characteristic divides it off from the practical thought of everyday life, from thinking in dreams, from religion, fantasy and art, the second marks a further line of cleavage from the thought of everyday life and at the same time from that of the specialized sciences, in so far as it is not philosophic. For interest in the individual sciences is built up of theoretical and practical components; hence, in so far as knowledge is not, for them, an end in itself, it arises from practical need; the thought is thus directed to practical ends and is preparatory, not self-sufficient.

The desire for knowledge gives rise to a form of thought which is not directed towards action but is sufficient in itself; from time to time, however, and in circumstances of which we are ignorant, other impulses can do the same, though normally they only impel to action and to preparatory thought. Then, in such unknown circumstances, these impulses may combine with the impulse for knowledge and beget philosophic interest and philosophic thought. But here we come once again to the question, the really difficult, increasingly insistent and burning question: what are these enigmatic circumstances? What is capable of diverting the life-impulses of man from action—and action is, after all, their *raison d'être*—and of constraining them into the mysterious paths of philosophic thought? The reason can only lie in the men themselves who behave thus; only the psychology of the philosophers can shed light on the psychology of philosophy. The theoretical philosopher must be a man who has something in him which prevents him from action: it is with this expectation in mind that we approach him.

CHAPTER VI

THE PSYCHOLOGY OF PRACTICAL PHILOSOPHY

PRACTICAL philosophy is the scientifically supported assertion, the propagation and the realization of life-ideals. What has this to do with theoretical philosophy? It is true that scientific thought plays an important part in it by seeking to justify the ideals and by pointing the way to their realization; but this form of thought is neither an aim nor is it an end in itself; nor again does it mark a pause, but it tends to action and furthers the cause of the conduct of life—in a word, it is not autarchic but preparatory thought. Hence the outstanding and essential characteristic of theoretical philosophy, the fact that it is both scientific and autarchic, does not apply to thought in practical philosophy. Does this mean that the apparent connexion between theoretical and practical philosophy does not after all exist, in spite of the common name, the constant feeling of its existence and the fact that it is implicit in the frequency with which both are found united in one person? Or, more exactly, that it is no closer than the connexion between mathematics, or other forms of scientific thought, and practical philosophy? We are loth to make this assumption for we can neither deny that thought in theoretical philosophy is autarchic nor that it is not so in practical philosophy.

Yet the existence of the connexion becomes clear when we look more closely into the functions of thought in practical philosophy. In the life and teaching of Socrates the absence of wants had already come to play its part as an ideal. To have no wants was an attribute of God, to have few was to approach divinity. If, however, the source of our actions is to be sought in wants, their absence will betoken a drying up of the source and must lead to a restriction of practical activity, as was in fact the case with Socrates. The cynics, too, professed and practised the ideal of having no wants. The more wants a man has the more difficult it is to satisfy them and the more he is exposed to the possibilities of suffering. If, therefore, he wishes to avoid suffering, he must reduce his wants to the lowest level compatible with maintaining life. This he does by making it a principle and practice to abstain from gratifying them. By thus rejecting material possessions, pleasure, honours and glory, however, powerful springs of action, as in the case of Socrates, are paralysed. Setting out from quite a different point, Aristippus comes to a similar conclusion. For him, the highest joys are those of the present moment; we should live in the moment and give ourselves entirely to its pleasures, for it is vain to prepare for a future that is not of our own making. But this very care for the future is one of the bases of human activity. To declare it to be useless is to advocate a life of indolence, of *dolce far niente* and of inactivity. Epicurus' ideal is life in undisturbed peace of mind. This calls for freedom from bodily pain and mental anxiety and for pleasure only in so far as it does not excite the emotions. Such a life of peace and joy is only open to those who have access to the good things of life which are available without undue struggle or worry and reject them when they can only be bought at the price of anxiety and pain. Thus Epicurus taught, and thus he lived, far from the turmoil of public and professional life, in peaceful surroundings, amongst friends, in the enjoyment of social, æsthetic and spiritual pleasures, resembling, in his freedom from all anxiety, his divinities who, in the interterrestrial spaces, lived the life of the soul far removed from earthly doings and disturbances. Here again, we have a teaching which is completely repugnant to action and to practical life with its incessant conflicts.

The case of the Stoics at first sight seems to be different, for their teaching expressly demands active work in the sphere allotted to every individual. And yet it is not difficult to find, even in this philosophy, tendencies which are inimical to action. The Stoic ideal is that of life at one with nature, *i.e.*, in the words of the Stoics themselves, a life which takes nature as its example and treats man as an image of the universe—a microcosm. And how does the Stoic regard the macrocosm which he takes as his example? As requiring nothing outside itself, as obeying immutable laws and as governed by reason. Thus, too, should men be—self-sufficient, immutable and governed by reason. Self-sufficiency, however, means that the soul is independent of health, beauty, wealth, women, children, friendship and honours—in a word, from everything which depends upon fate and not upon ourselves. All these things are regarded by the Stoic as not being goods; he enjoys them if he has them but he does not strive to obtain them if they are absent and he wastes no time in regret if he loses them. By thus disparaging all the most important goods of life, powerful springs of the will are naturally hindered in their action; hence, once again, we are faced with tendencies which are anti-practical and inhibit action.

Tendencies of this kind are still stronger in the neo-Platonic system. The neo-Platonic ideal is union with God attained through ecstatic transport: such psychic conditions of the soul are, however, incompatible with practical life and those who cultivate them become incapable of action. This, however, does not trouble the neo-Platonist, since, in his belief, action cannot bring him any nearer to his mystic goal.

And, as the fetters of the Middle Ages gradually worked loose and the modern era with its wonderful discoveries began to stimulate the lust for action, Geulinx announced that weariest of all philosophies of life which is contained in the sentence: *Ubi nihil vales, ibi nihil velis*—" where thou canst not avail thou shouldst not attempt "—a sentence which declares all action in the physical world to be impossible.

Spinoza's ideal in life is the intellectual love of God, *i.e.*, the merging of self in the cosmos and belief in the inevitability of all events which free mankind from the rule of the emotions and thereby fill him with love of the omnipotent divine being. Here again, we have a quietistic motive approaching that of the neo-Platonists.

This tendency is, however, particularly clear in Schopenhauer's ideal of deliverance from existence through denial of the will to live. Here is a quite definite call for the renunciation of all satisfaction of impulse and all activity of the will, with a view to the complete extinction of individuality.

All these examples show how thought in practical philosophy serves the expression of quietistic tendencies which offer obstacles to action; whether the life-ideal is called happiness, freedom from wants, life in harmony with nature or pleasure, union with God, or deliverance, it serves everywhere to impede action and to justify inactivity. So far, therefore, the thought underlying practical philosophy is inhibitive thought.

It would, however, be a mistake to think that there is no place in practical philosophy for thought which incites to action. We find it in the life-ideals of Fichte, Hartmann and Nietzsche, though in practical philosophy as a whole it is greatly outweighed by inhibitive thought.

Thus, practical philosophic thought consists of inhibitive and of inciting thought—the two kinds which we have recognized above as forms of determinative thought—with a remarkable preponderance of the former.

Let us recall to mind what we have already said as to the psychological roots of theoretical philosophy—that it presupposed some kind of obstacle to the translation of impulses into action. And now, in practical philosophy, we find a predominance of inhibitive thought which also results in a restraint upon action. May we not find in this the connexion between theoretical and practical philosophy for which we are looking? One thing, however, still stands in our way: there is, in practical philosophy, not only a form of thought which tends to inhibit action, but also a form which, on the contrary, incites to it. In seeking a solution of this difficulty we may advance an idea which must for the present remain only a conjecture, viz., that not only the life-ideals which inhibit action but also those which stimulate it are only found in individuals who suffer from an impediment to action. The inhibitive ones would represent the expression of the inhibitive tendencies and the inciting ones both the resistance to these tendencies and the expression of the impulses urging towards action. Determinative thought, we may say in support of this conjecture, only occurs when an impulse to action is impeded by an opposing tendency; otherwise action, and not merely thought, ensues. Practical philosophizing is however, in so far as it is thinking at all, determinative thinking; thus it presupposes that action is impeded.

The connexion between theoretical and practical philosophy is therefore a psychological one residing in their common origin. It is the inhibition of action which causes the life-impulses to be diverted into thought—autarchic thought, theoretical philosophy—instead of being converted into action. It is, again, to overcome an obstacle to action that men need ideals which urge them on or to bear it that they need quietistic ones—determinative thought, practical philosophy. The practical philosopher, too, must be a man who has something in him which prevents him from action and it is with this expectation in mind that we approach him.

CHAPTER VII

METHOD

It is easy to prove that " the Germans " are militaristic, " the Jews " indifferent in religious matters, and "artists" sexually uncontrolled; it is not much more difficult to prove the contrary. Recipe: take suitable individuals, actions, omissions or assertions and ignore the opposite ones or declare them to be exceptions which prove the rule.

Are " philosophers " men who are in some way impeded from action? It is true that Socrates, Epicurus, Malebranche, Spinoza, Stirner and Nietzsche did not show much activity in practical life; they neither pursued a practical profession nor ran after money or women, and they took no part in politics; they seem, rather, to have justified the famous saying of Pythagoras that philosophers are lookers-on in the game of life, taking no part in its struggles and following no occupation. But was not Descartes an officer and Bacon a statesman? Did not Hume and Schopenhauer show energy in respectively making and keeping their fortunes? St Augustine, Rousseau, and Schopenhauer were, in matters erotic, far from mere lookers-on; Plato, Leibniz, and Mill were zealous politicians. We only need compose another saying and the philosophers will be seen to be patterns of energy and alertness.

But how are we to avoid the mistake which is inherent in such a biased selection of material if, as is the case, we must after all make some selection? I know only one way; the examples must be selected from a completely different standpoint from that of their suitability for what we want to prove.

For the purposes of the psychology of the philosophers we need not seek this standpoint far afield; let us take the philosophers *par excellence*, the kings among them, the great philosophers—the standard of greatness being the usually accepted one of a combination of originality and historic influence.[1] I have drawn up a list of thirty names, amongst which there will naturally be one or other whose right to inclusion will be contested whilst the omission of others may for many be a cause of surprise; the majority, however, are hardly in doubt. In the following pages only these thirty will be quoted and only their lives will be investigated, in order to ascertain whether they really contained some strange psychic anomaly—that form of inactivity, that inhibition of action, which we conjectured to be a prerequisite of philosophic thought. But in no circumstances will other thinkers, tempting though they may appear, be quoted in evidence; for, since a negative case may be found for every positive one, we should merely be manufacturing testimony of the kind which we have decided to reject. Here is the list of our thirty philosophers, arranged according to the date of their birth: Socrates, Plato,

[1] H. Gompertz defines (p. 92) a great man as "one whose most essential personal characteristics meet the demands of his time." This seems to me too restrictive; they may also meet the requirements of a later time, as in the case of Spinoza and Stirner.

Aristotle, Epicurus, St Augustine, Bruno, Bacon, Hobbes, Descartes, Locke, Spinoza, Malebranche, Leibniz, Berkeley, Hume, Rousseau, Kant, Fichte, Hegel, Schelling, Herbart, Schopenhauer, Comte, Fechner, Feuerbach, Mill, Stirner, Spencer, Hartmann, and Nietzsche.

CHAPTER VIII

PROFESSION

PROFESSION is the name given to an occupation consistently pursued for the purpose of gain. This definition does not exclude interest in the professional work; but an occupation pursued solely from interest and without any purpose of gain is not a profession but a hobby; it is one of the two forms of occupation distinct from professional occupation. The other is an occupation which, although pursued for purposes of gain, is only temporary, *e.g.*, the giving of private lessons before finding a professional post as doctor or chemist.

The great majority of people regard their profession as something immensely important—and rightly, for it supplies the means of existence for them and their families and thereby constitutes the material basis of their whole lives. Consequently, they try as early as possible—in fact, as soon as the period of study judged essential is over—to secure a foothold in a profession; if something advantageous is offered them, they accept it and, apart from short periods of recreation, they continue in their profession uninterruptedly for decades—even for life; they do not change it without some urgent reason of health or finance and they leave it only when they have grown old and have made provision for themselves.

From necessity and practice they gradually acquire a more or less high degree of skill both in their professional duties proper and in their relations with colleagues and superiors.

Thus, early entry into the profession, acceptance of offers, no long breaks, no change of profession, its abandonment only late in life and professional suitability in the sense just mentioned—these six qualifications give a rough picture of the ordinary or normal [1] attitude towards professional life.

Let us compare it with the professional lives of our philosophers:

Socrates lived on the yield of a small capital sum, without following any profession.

Plato studied and travelled until his fortieth year and then founded the Academy. At 60 he broke off his teaching in order to engage in politics at Syracuse; he did so again five years later.

Aristotle, until the age of 38 Plato's pupil and three years later Alexander's tutor, founded his school at the age of 50.

Epicurus, who was also at first a teacher, had already begun to teach at 35

St Augustine was a teacher of rhetoric for ten years, then he was made a presbyter against his will and shortly afterwards, again in spite of grave doubts on his part, a

[1] The notion of "normal," as used here and elsewhere in the book is simply that of "ordinary" or rather "most frequently observed." When, on the other hand, I speak of the "normal" man, I do so chiefly only because the word "ordinary" has a subsidiary disparaging sense [*in German—Trs.*]. Subsequently, however, it will be seen that the "ordinary" man is in practical life the "normal" one, too, in the sense of being the "fittest" or the "best adapted."

bishop; this office he held until his death thirty-five years later.

Bruno was a monk for thirteen years and had many conflicts with his companions and superiors. Then he became a private teacher, then a proof-corrector, then for two years a professor in Toulouse; for five years he lectured in Paris and for two years in Wittenberg. He made himself insupportable through his rudeness in all these places. He was later a private teacher at Zürich, Padua and Venice.

Bacon at the age of 36 was a Queen's Counsel extraordinary, an unpaid office. The office of Attorney-General, for which he had previously been a candidate, was not given to him and his ensuing candidature for another high office of State also failed owing to his parliamentary activities which displeased the Queen; at 36 he had no practice, no paid office, but heavy debts. Not until seven years later was he paid for his duties as Counsel; at 46 he received his first State appointment, at 52 he was Attorney-General—the office for which he had striven twenty years earlier, four years later he became Keeper of the Great Seal, and finally, a year afterwards, Lord Chancellor. But only three years later he was overthrown for taking bribes as a judge, and he lost all his offices.

Hobbes was a tutor at 20, then a private secretary until the age of 30. At 43, he again became a teacher. After a further interval—lasting this time for five years—he accepted a post as tutor to the Prince of Wales, but retained it only for a year. For the last thirty years of his life he was without a profession.

Descartes became a soldier at 21; four years later he gave up this career, upon which he always looked back with disgust. He sold his belongings. He made no attempt to obtain the post of commissariat officer in the army which was open to him and refused the offer of a judgeship.

Locke, at 33, was a secretary of embassy. He refused a further similar post, and an ecclesiastical office. The degree of doctor of medicine which he endeavoured to obtain at the age of 34 was not granted to him because he refused to sit for the requisite examination. He thereupon entered the service of Lord Shaftesbury as doctor, tutor and assistant, and remained for nine years. For reasons of health he then spent four years in France, again finding occupation as a tutor. For the following three years he was again a collaborator of Lord Shaftesbury, after whose death he engaged in literary pursuits for six years. He refused an ambassadorship which was then offered him, but, at the urgent instance of the King, he accepted the post of Judge of Appeal, because practically no work was associated with it. Seven years later he was made Trade Commissioner, entirely against his wishes, but he asked to be relieved of the post after a few months since he wished for leisure and was disgusted by the ugly experiences of the corruption of the time which his office brought with it; his request was, however, refused. In the year following he refused a diplomatic post and three years later, at the age of 68, he retired from his position as Trade Commissioner although the King had permitted him to live permanently in the country, so long as he remained in touch with the Board.

Spinoza made his living by grinding lenses, but what he earned thereby was not sufficient even for his own derisory needs, so that several friends made him allowances. Nevertheless he refused a call to Heidelberg as professor of philosophy

Malebranche spent his life as an Oratorian priest in scientific work.

Leibniz, at 21, refused a professorship at Altdorf. Four years later he became Comptroller to the Elector of Mainz and at the same time acted outside his office as tutor and teacher. At 27 he gave up these posts in order to study for four years. He then became counsellor and librarian to the Hanoverian Court. Besides these duties he conducted mining work, which he gave up, however, after six years. From the age of 39 he was historian to the House of Brunswick. He refused Imperial service in Vienna and a post as custodian of the Vatican library. The displeasure of the Elector was aroused by his frequent journeys, which led to continual interruption of his historical work. He founded the Academy of Science in Berlin and became its president. This duplication of posts in Hanover and Berlin made his position increasingly difficult, particularly as, in spite of twenty years' work, he published nothing of the history of the House of Brunswick which he had undertaken to write.

Berkeley was first a chaplain, then a secretary for a year, and for five years the travelling companion of a bishop's son. At 39 he became a Dean and four years later he went to America to found a college. After three years of wasted effort he returned and became at 49 Bishop of Cloyne.

Hume studied first law and then philosophy. He wished later to enter business but gave up the attempt after a few months. At 26 he had no post and had made no attempt to obtain one. At 33 he was a candidate for the Chair of Philosophy at Edinburgh but failed to obtain it; he then became tutor to a marquis but felt extremely unhappy in the post and was dismissed after a year. For a year he was Secretary to General St Clair. At 40 he again failed to obtain a Chair,[1] at Glasgow, but was shortly afterwards made Keeper of the Advocates' Library at Edinburgh. After five years he resigned in order to pursue literary work exclusively. At 52, after a preliminary refusal, he accepted the offer of the British Ambassador to France to accompany him as secretary. Four years later he was Under-Secretary of State, but after a year and a half he resigned, in order to spend the rest of his life at ease.

Rousseau was first a clerk; he was dismissed and became an engraver's apprentice but ran away at the age of 16. Then he became a lackey and a clerk. He was again dismissed and entered a seminary, from which he was expelled after two months. His next occupation, of which he understood nothing, was that of singing-master and composer; then he became secretary to an adventurer and, after his exposure, teacher. He very soon abandoned this position and, at the age of 20, became a Survey official. This he only endured for two years, when he became a music-teacher again. A neurasthenic affection obliged him to abandon this occupation after a short time. Having passed five years without occupation,

[1] [Of Logic—*Trs.*].

he again became a teacher, but after a year his longing for his sweetheart brought him back to her side. Serious quarrels with his chief lost him a further post as Secretary of Embassy after holding it for a very short time. He then lived as an opera librettist, again became a secretary and finally cashier to a tax-collector, a remunerative position at last. But the large sums of money entrusted to him deprived him of his peace of mind and he gave up this post in turn although he regarded himself as morally obliged to provide for his mistress and her family. So at the age of 37, he became a copyist of music. Though this brought in but little money, he refused a position on the *Journal des Savants* with a good salary, fearing that he would have insufficient leisure. His attitude was the same when, seven years later, he was offered a post as librarian at Geneva. He continued to live by copying music.

Kant was a private tutor for nine years. His performances in this sphere fell short of his expectations. At 31 he obtained the right to lecture at a university. He refused a Chair of Literature and several offers to go abroad. At 46 he at last became professor-in-ordinary of philosophy

Fichte was also a private tutor for ten years. Various attempts which he made during this time to live by writing proved abortive. At 32 he became a professor at Jena where he very soon caused scandal by arranging for his lectures to coincide with the church service on Sunday; later, he became involved in a quarrel with a students' association. Only a year after assuming office he was granted leave of absence on this account. After five years he was dismissed for atheism, a measure due to his tactless and challenging attitude towards the government. At 43 he was made professor at Erlangen, where he had little success. Five years later he became rector of Berlin University but soon quarrelled with his colleagues and resigned after six months.

Hegel was a private tutor for seven years, then a lecturer at Jena for six. After a year and a half as editor of a newspaper he became head master of a school at 36. At 44 he was made professor at Heidelberg and two years later at Berlin, where he continued with great success until his death

Schelling was a private tutor for three years only and at 23 was already a professor at Jena. He had little success and soon quarrelled with his colleagues. After five years he was made professor-in-ordinary at Würzburg. His attacks upon the government led to a severe reprimand which he accepted, cowed. Three years later he went to Munich as general secretary of the Academy of Graphic and Plastic Art and later became secretary of the Academy of Science there. His stay lasted for sixteen years, interrupted by a visit of one year to Erlangen where he announced his intention of delivering lectures, though he actually delivered but few. He then returned to Munich as professor. After a further period of fourteen years he became professor in Berlin where, two years later, he gave up lecturing altogether because his complaint regarding the printing of a lecture failed to receive satisfaction.

Herbart was a tutor and teacher for six years. At 26 he became lecturer at Göttingen, where he was successful.

He was later called to Königsberg to occupy Kant's Chair; after twenty-four years he went to Göttingen for the second time.

Schopenhauer was for two years a commercial apprentice; he then studied philosophy. At 32 he had acquired the right to lecture at Berlin university, but only did so for one term. No subsequent lectures were delivered because he arranged them for a time which clashed with Hegel's. Eight years later a second attempt to become a lecturer failed. Receiving a discouraging reply, he gave the plan up for good and devoted himself at leisure to his philosophical work

Comte began by being secretary to a banker for three weeks and lived subsequently by giving private lessons. He then collaborated with Saint-Simon, but left him after six years and attempted to gain a living by literary work. This was interrupted by a severe mental illness. After his recovery Comte made numerous abortive attempts to enter a profession. Finally, at 34, he became coach and examiner at the *Ecole Polytechnique* in Paris. An attempt to obtain a professorship in Paris failed. As the result of his attacks upon the management of the school he lost his post after twelve years and failed to obtain another. He lived thereafter chiefly on his friends' charity.

Fechner lived at first by his literary work; at 22 he became a lecturer, then a professor of physics, but had to give up this work owing to severe neurasthenia. After his cure, he preferred not to resume it but lectured in philosophy.

Feuerbach, who was at first a *privatdozent* at Erlangen, barred his own path to advancement by his work on

Death and Immortality. He therefore relinquished his lectorship, devoting himself in the first place to literature alone, and later to lectures as well. His candidature for professorships failed repeatedly. In spite of great destitution he could not reconcile himself even to working on a newspaper for any considerable length of time.

Mill was an official of India House for thirty-five years, a position which he regarded as recreation from his scientific work. At 50 he was chief of the office. When, two years later the East India Company was dissolved, he was offered a post as adviser to the Secretary of State for India but refused it and devoted himself thenceforward to literature only.

Stirner was for five years a teacher at a girls' high school. When his work, *Der Einzige und sein Eigentum*, had been sent to press, he gave up his position, convinced that he would be dismissed as soon as it became public. Later, he attempted to open a milk business and, after its failure, carried on various agencies, with the result that his distress became increasingly great.

Spencer was a teacher for three months, an engineer for three years, an editor for a month and an engineer again for two years. Two years later he again became an editor but four years afterwards relinquished this important and well-paid post, which left him considerable leisure, because of a small legacy which, added to his savings, left him independent for the time being. Five years later he was almost without means and his friends tried to find him a position. Spencer, however, refused the posts offered, partly for political reasons and partly for fear that his time would be wasted. He lived on legacies and subscriptions until his fifty-sixth year, after which he derived an adequate income from his writings.

Hartmann began his career as an officer, but had to resign owing to a severe contusion of the knee-cap. After he had tried painting and music, he at last found satisfaction in philosophy. He refused three offers of professorships on the ground of physical suffering and the wish for independence.

Nietzsche was, at 24, professor of philosophy at Basel; after five years he was already finding the burden heavy. At 32 a nervous complaint forced him to abandon part of his duties and two years later he relinquished his professorship entirely.

If this account has been a somewhat monotonous one, this is due not only to the multiplicity of dates but in no small part to the frequent recurrence of certain expressions such as "refused," "relinquished," and "failed." But it is this very monotony that interests us, for it is due to the fact that the philosophers almost without exception gave proof in their professional lives of an attitude diverging conspicuously from the normal.

We find :—

Late beginnings in the case of Plato, who founded his school at 40, and Aristotle, who only founded his at 50.

Refusals.—St Augustine resisted nomination as Bishop; Descartes refused the posts of army Commissariat Officer and Judge; Locke various diplomatic posts; Spinoza a call to Heidelberg; Leibniz imperial service and the librarianship at the Vatican; Rousseau the post on the *Journal des Savants* and the librarianship at Geneva; Kant the professorship of literature and a series of calls to Halle, Jena, Erlangen, Mitau, and Halle again; Fechner the resumption of his teaching of physics; Mill a high office of State; Spencer also several offices of State; and Hartmann three calls to academic posts.

Long Interruptions.—Plato went twice to Sicily in order to put his political ideas into practice; Leibniz continually broke off his historical work for the sake of other enterprises; Hobbes, Locke, Hume, Rousseau, Schelling, Comte, and Spencer allowed long periods of leisure to intervene between their professional labours; Spinoza must have conducted his lens-grinding with considerable interruptions for he would otherwise have earned more in view of the excellence of his glasses.

Changes.—In the case of the majority, these were frequent, in some cases to the point of instability: St Augustine was a teacher of rhetoric for ten years before he became a priest; Bruno was a monk, a private teacher, a printer's proof-corrector, a professor, and again a private teacher; Hobbes was a tutor, private secretary, and tutor again; Locke was a secretary, doctor, tutor, politician and State official consecutively or concurrently; Berkeley gave up his excellent post as Dean after only four years in order to spread Christianity and civilization in America; Hume was a business man, tutor, secretary, librarian, Secretary of Embassy and Under-Secretary of State. We may also point to Rousseau's chaos of careers; to Hegel who was lecturer, editor, schoolmaster, and professor; to Stirner who was teacher, milk-dealer, and agent; and to Spencer who several times alternated between teacher, engineer, and editor. Hobbes, Descartes, Schopenhauer, Feuerbach, Spencer, Hartmann, and Nietzsche abandoned their professions early and permanently, Socrates appears never to have had one, and Spencer was only for a short time beyond the reach of material need.

Tactless or Offensive Conduct.—Bruno aroused general hatred by his rough and aggressive manner; Bacon accepted gifts in the conduct of his office; Leibniz made himself unpopular by neglect of his work, by frequent absences, and by entertaining relations with other Courts; Rousseau could not settle down in any profession; Fichte and Schelling came into collision with colleagues and governors; Schopenhauer arranged his lectures to clash with Hegel's; Comte lost his position by attacking the directors of the *Ecole Polytechnique;* Feuerbach barred his own career at its commencement by his work on *Death and Immortality;* and Stirner ruined his by his preposterous milk business.

Repeated failure in Candidatures and Attempts to enter Professions.—Hume, Schopenhauer, Comte, Feuerbach, and Stirner may be cited in this connexion. Progress was slow in the case of Berkeley, who only became a Bishop at 49, and of Kant and Hegel who became professors-in-ordinary at 46 and 44.

In the foregoing summary only three of our list are not mentioned and may thus be regarded as not differing from the average in the matter of profession: Epicurus, Malebranche, and Herbart. Even so it is doubtful whether Epicurus and Malebranche ever exercised one.

Result.—The overwhelming majority of the great philosophers—twenty-seven out of thirty—display in the matter of profession conspicuous divergencies of various kinds from the normal. All these—whether late beginnings, refusals, interruptions, changes, early relinquishment of careers, failures in candidatures, clashes with colleagues and superiors, or slow advancement—can be brought under two heads, viz., hesitation to embark upon a career and inefficiency in it when embarked upon. To be career-shy is not, of course, to be work-shy, the philosophers performed the work which befitted them —philosophic thinking—with the greatest intensity. The majority also succeeded in writing down their thoughts; many indeed have written enormously. Peculiarities, and some occur in this connexion also, will be dealt with later in the chapter on inhibition. For the moment we will be content to say, in summing up, that the philosophers were for the most part diffident in and unsuited for a professional life.

CHAPTER IX

MONEY

Money is generally earned by professional work, and in so far as this is the case, the attitude of the philosophers towards it was already ripe for discussion in the foregoing chapter; but it may also be obtained as a gift. However obtained, it can be either put to use and increased or it can be expended, and all these points touch upon aspects of the money-complex which are independent of the exercise of a profession; hence we will consider the complex by itself.

In order to have a standard of comparison, let us consider firstly the attitude of the normal person: for him, money is a quite special thing, one of the chief and governing considerations in life. A large part, generally indeed the largest part, of his thoughts and desires is focussed upon earning money. This being the case, it is not surprising that in normal conditions nearly every one succeeds in putting himself into a position to earn his living. If there is a surplus, something is usually put aside and the savings—like money which is received in other ways, *e.g.*, through inheritance—is kept for an emergency or to be used as capital in further enterprises. The normal person has, as a rule, little money to spare for the support of others—at all events, for their support to any great extent. If, therefore, firstly the will and secondly the capacity to earn, thirdly the conservation of property, and fourthly the slightness of the desire to share it with others characterize the normal being, we shall not find many normal beings amongst our philosophers.

It is true that we hear of Hume that he was very eager to earn money; St Augustine mentions the hankering after riches as one of the vices of his youth, Leibniz was eager to increase his income and Bacon accepted gifts even as a judge. But by far the majority of the great thinkers had very little desire for money; in fact, where anything approaching a safe competency was available—and sometimes even when it was not—they had no such desire at all. Plato observed this when, in the *Republic*, he characterized the philosopher as "free from covetousness." Socrates took no money for his teaching and followed no other calling, living in grinding poverty on a tiny capital. In his lawsuit he gave the fine which he was able to pay as a mina or less than £4. Epicurus also asked no fees of his scholars; he accepted voluntary gifts but only to the extent to which he had need of them. Descartes, whose private income was sufficient to support him, refused to engage in any calling. Spinoza, whose spectacle glasses were much sought after, was not able to earn even the 12 kreutzers (2½d.) daily which he needed to live. He refused a present of 2000 gulden from his friend de Vries and also refused to be made his sole heir. He reduced to 300 the 500 gulden set aside for him yearly. He refused the 200 gulden which de Witt had set aside for him, because the heirs made difficulties; he also refused his father's inheritance. Rousseau, in spite of oppressive poverty, took money matters with so little seriousness that he did not even ask for his fee for collaborating in the *Encyclopédie* and could not make up his mind to present himself to the King, who wished to grant him a pension. Hume wrote that Rousseau was so popular and so greatly admired in Paris that millions of francs could have been collected for him in a fortnight, but Rousseau would accept nothing. Feuerbach, even when in the greatest need, refused to contribute to periodicals because he could not prevail upon himself to write for money. Spencer at once gave up his position as an editor, as soon as his means were assured for a short time owing to a small legacy, in order to devote himself undisturbed to the development of his thoughts.

The capacity of the great thinkers to earn money was for the most part even smaller than their will. There are only two exceptions: Bacon, who earned more than £2500 per annum as Chancellor, and Hume whose fortune grew from the smallest beginnings to over £50,000. But over against these two there stands a compact mass of less fortunate ones. Bruno, for example, after his flight from the monastery, was always in needy circumstances which, by means of private lessons, essays, lectures and proof-correcting, he managed to allay, though never for long. Hobbes, too, never earned more than a modest income; his small landed property brought him in less than £20, and he drew £50 a year so long as he remained with the Devonshire family; for the rest he lived on pensions and legacies derived from his friends and from the King. Locke was in a similar position and lived most of his life in very humble circumstances; this may have contributed to the reasons which kept him from marrying. Rousseau did not earn enough by his music-copying and his literary work to lift him out of the most burdensome poverty. Fichte lived in his youth in extremely straitened circumstances. At 30 he was again entirely without means and was obliged to approach Kant for a loan. Hegel was until a mature age in deplorable difficulties; he begged his publisher to advance him money on his *Phänomenologie des Geistes;* even his marriage was nearly postponed owing to lack of funds, though it was decided upon late enough—at 41. Schopenhauer's extraordinary tenacity in holding on to his fortune was due, as he recognised, to his very inability to earn. Comte, in spite of the greatest efforts, was unable to find any position worthy of the name until he was appointed to the *Ecole Polytechnique* at 34; after his dismissal he had to depend on money subscribed for him. In him, inability to earn was combined with complete incomprehension of money matters. After his attacks on the management of the *Ecole Polytechnique* had cost him his appointment, Mill obtained for him a present of 6000 francs. Comte drew from this the conclusion that he would be provided for until he found a position—with the natural result that Mill left him alone. His will provided that pensions for life should be paid to his wife, his servant, and others; he also gave instructions that his house should be preserved intact as a memorial. But considerable debts were all that was left for the carrying out of these instructions. Stirner's enterprises succeeded only in rapidly exhausting his wife's fortune, and when left to his own resources he soon found himself in the bitterest need and was twice imprisoned for debt.

The philosophers cut a better figure when it comes to saving money and preserving fortunes already in existence. Thus, Plato probably lived on his private means, in so far as they were not spent on travelling. He was not rich and had to borrow the large sums which he was called upon to advance on behalf of Dionysius. Descartes lived entirely upon the income from his capital. Hume was extremely thrifty and by far the best financier amongst the philosophers—indeed the only one. Kant, though in receipt of only a modest income, became in time well-to-do and was able to buy a house. Schopenhauer adroitly rescued his capital from his debtor's shipwreck and succeeded, although he depended upon it almost exclusively, in adding to it.

But among the great thinkers there were also some reckless men who wasted their capital without any forethought, some unwise ones who lost it, and some spendthrifts who could not live on a large income. Thus Comte, after his marriage, adopted the simple plan of living on his wife's money, as also did Stirner, who subsequently lost it in business undertakings. Leibniz also falls within this category, for he was careless with money and allowed himself to be cheated by mechanics and servants. And finally Bacon, who had already been arrested for debt in his youth, remained a spendthrift; he spent £10,000 in building Verulam House and gave a gratuity of £50 to one of the King's servants.

This leads us to the subject of generosity, of which we hear numerous reports in the lives of our philosophers. Hobbes gave his small property to his brother; he also gave his nephew £200 to redeem a mortgage, and he was so ready to furnish assistance in other matters that people were at a complete loss to understand how he could reconcile this attitude with his materialism. Locke assisted the poor as far as it lay in his power and his principle was to go beyond what was absolutely necessary, to the extent of ensuring the comfort of his protégés. Spinoza, who lived with the utmost frugality himself, was as generous as if he had money beyond his needs. Of Hume his friend Adam Smith says that his great thriftiness never prevented him from giving with both hands when the occasion required, even when his own affairs were at their worst. Rousseau, in spite of his very small income, sent nearly one-third of it, 350 francs, to Geneva for the relief of destitution. Kant, again, supported his relatives and other needy persons to a generous extent; he placed 500 thalers at the disposal of a friend for a journey to be undertaken for the purpose of study; they were, however, not accepted. Schopenhauer supported his relatives and also spent much money for other charitable purposes. It is therefore not true that he was merely a theoretical advocate of charity. Nietzsche, who himself was dependent upon a paltry pension of 2000 francs, not only expended a substantial portion of it upon the support of his sister but also lent to strangers money which he naturally did not see again.

Let us strike the balance. Among the great thinkers, one, Hume, was a capable financier; of Kant, Schelling,

Herbart, Fechner, Mill, and Hartmann we know that they behaved in money matters like the general run of men; of Aristotle, St Augustine, Malebranche and Berkeley nothing to the contrary is at all events known. The remaining nineteen, however, display a more or less conspicuous divergency from normal behaviour in respect of either the will or the capacity to earn money, which expresses itself in a careless attitude towards their possessions or in conspicuous generosity. Since the two last-mentioned characteristics also point to a diminution or inhibition of the impulse to earn money, we may state our conclusion by saying that the majority of philosophers were either unwilling to earn money or incapable of doing so.

CHAPTER X

LOVE AND MARRIAGE

SEXUAL relations with the opposite sex are so customary a thing in men up to the threshold of senility that if they are absent throughout life or given up at an early age, there is strong reason to suspect bodily or mental abnormality. In normal men there is, moreover, a very strong tendency to stabilize these relations at some time or other in the form of marriage; economic considerations, loneliness, and the desire for children also foster marriage, and the combined result of all these factors is that the overwhelming majority of men do marry. I am happily in a position to give exact statistics. Of the male population aged forty and above, the proportion of bachelors was[1] :—

Country	1890	1910
Germany	8·3 %	8·0 %
Netherlands	12·3 %	11·9 %
England	10·1 %	11·5 %
Italy	12·0 %	10·3 %
France	11·6 %	9·8 %

There was no noticeable change in these figures during the nineteenth century and, as we have no reason to

[1] Conrad, 4. 1, 5th impression, 1923, p. 98.

suppose that they were different in previous centuries, we may regard it as a fact that about 90 per cent. of men marry.

A third and important characteristic of normal behaviour is seen in the age at which marriage is contracted; by far the greater number of men marry before the age of 40, though the actual age depends on racial, social, and professional factors. Thus, in the year 1900, of all men who married, the percentage aged over 40 was: Germany, 7·2 per cent.; Austria, 11·6 per cent.; Holland, 9·1 per cent.; Belgium, 8·0 per cent.; England, 8·2 per cent.; Ireland, 9·2 per cent.; France, 7·9 per cent.; Italy, 10·1 per cent.—an average of not more than 8·9 per cent.[1]

Fourthly and finally, we would mention the degree of stability attained in the majority of marriages. Divorces have, it is true, been numerous in the last few years, especially in the upper social classes; they were, however, in earlier days—and it is to these, after all, that we must turn for our standards of comparison—much less common; in the year 1890, at all events, out of 12,700,000 men over twenty years old in Germany, 8,400,000 were married, and only 25,000, or about 0·3 per cent., were divorced.[2]

The proportions among our philosophers are, however, quite different. We know with some degree of certainty that Plato and Malebranche never had sexual relations with women owing, in the case of Plato, to homosexuality, and in that of Malebranche to a physical condition resulting from an operation performed in his youth for

[1] Conrad, 4. 1, p. 138.

[2] *Idem*, p. 138.

stone. In regard to Spinoza, we are entitled to assume from the complete silence of all sources of information on this point that there is nothing to report, for the zeal which his adversaries displayed in trying to discover any and every scandal in his life would hardly have made it possible to overlook a matter of this kind. St Augustine separated at the age of 33 from the woman with whom he had cohabited, and he lived a life of complete chastity thereafter. As a child and young man, Rousseau displayed perverse, masochistic and exhibitionistic tendencies; he was unable to shake off the habit of onanism during his whole life and at about fifty he gave up all sexual relations.

Otherwise we are, naturally enough, without much information about the sex life of the philosophers. We only know that St Augustine, Descartes and Schopenhauer had mistresses; the same is reported of Epicurus and Hobbes, but its truth is doubtful, as the reports are of a slanderous kind.

Attention has been drawn by Schopenhauer, and with special emphasis by Nietzsche, to the remarkable phenomenon that numerous great philosophers were unmarried. "Up to the present what great philosophers have been married?" Nietzsche asks. "Heraclitus, Plato, Descartes, Spinoza, Leibniz, Kant, Schopenhauer—they were not married, and, further, one cannot *imagine* them as married. A married philosopher belongs to *comedy*, that is my rule; as for that exception of a Socrates—the malicious Socrates married himself, it seems, *ironice*, just to prove this *very* rule."[1] Nietzsche exaggerates; in

[1] *The Genealogy of Morals*, 3rd Essay, § 7.

point of fact a number of great thinkers were married, in particular—besides Socrates—Aristotle, Bacon, Berkeley, Rousseau, Fichte, Hegel, Schelling, Herbart, Comte, Fechner, Feuerbach, Mill, Stirner, and Hartmann—and Aristotle, Schelling, Stirner, and Hartmann even married twice. But, as is typical of Nietzsche, his exaggeration has a kernel of truth: of all men, 90 per cent. marry, but of our philosophers only 50 per cent. did so, and this points therefore unmistakably to their failure to follow the general rule.

This is still more noticeable when we come to look more closely into the marriages of the 50 per cent. The overwhelming majority of men, amounting in the civilized European states mentioned above to an average of 91 per cent., marry for the first time before the age of 40. But of our 15 philosophers no fewer than 6 married after 40—to wit, Socrates, whose age at marriage[1] we do not know exactly but of whose three sons at the time of his death, at 70, one was a youth and two were still children, Bacon, who married at 45, and Berkeley, who married at 43. Rousseau was 56 before he regularized his union of twenty-five years' standing with his mistress. Hegel, too, took a long time for reflexion. He was greatly worried to know whether he was fitted for happiness at all and especially for married happiness; finally, at 41, he took the decisive step. Mill married, after a friendship

[1] Gompertz (p. 57) puts it at about 55, but this can only be regarded as a maximum, for it presupposes that the eldest son was born immediately after wedlock, and was only fifteen when his father died. He might, however, only have been born after several years of childless marriage, or again there may have been elder children who died; finally, he may well have been older than 15. The only certainty is therefore that Socrates was well over forty when he married.

lasting for twenty years, when he was nearly 45. Thus 40 per cent. of such philosophers as married at all only made up their minds to do so when they were over 40, whilst the corresponding percentage for the generality of men is only 9

A not inconsiderable number of the philosophers' marriages followed an unhappy course. Socrates' misery is proverbial. Bacon's wife, whom he disinherited, was, according to certain of his allusions, unfaithful; after Bacon's death she married one of his former servants, who was presumably her lover. Comte also lived on bad terms with his wife; in a letter to Mill he calls his marriage civil war and an incessant duel and finally, after seventeen years, they separated. Stirner's case is similar but the conflict was much shorter and led to separation after three years, followed a few years later by divorce. Thus, of 15 marriages, 4 were unhappy and 2 led to separation—an enormous percentage in comparison with that given above of 0·3 per cent.

In sum—the married life of the philosophers shows conspicuous peculiarities; 15 out of 30 did not marry at all, 6 married very late, 4 were unhappy, 2 separated—and 7 remain of whom there is nothing particular to report. The philosophers, we must conclude, are mostly diffident about, or unsuited for, marriage.

CHAPTER XI

SOCIAL INTERCOURSE

MAN is a social animal; not, it is true, to the same extent as bees and ants, which perish if obliged to live alone, but still to the point of feeling, in general, very unhappy in such circumstances. Nor is he usually satisfied to live entirely in the circle of his own family and household but he extends his social relations further afield—to neighbours, colleagues, and to other people of his own kind. A certain amount of tolerance and give-and-take is essential for establishing good relations with our fellowmen; this we find in the general run of men and where it is not rooted in their character it is assured by the accepted rules of social intercourse which all men obey and gradually learn to practise. This naturally applies only as a general rule, but it *is* at all events a general rule. It is, for instance, a conspicuous trait to tend towards solitude, fall foul of everybody, or behave in the presence of others in a clumsy or unconventional way. Thus, the average man is social in the sense, (1) that he is inclined to foregather with others, (2) that he follows this inclination, (3) that he is more or less easy to get on with, and (4) that he accommodates himself to social conventions.

Let us see how the philosophers stand in this regard.

There are very few of the great thinkers whose behaviour was quite normal in all these things. Epicurus stands out as a man for whom friendship was one of the greatest goods and his whole life was spent amongst his friends; Hobbes is also depicted as a sociable man, a man of the world who always maintained relations with numerous learned and influential persons; Kant, Hegel, Herbart, and Hartmann were by inclination and practice thoroughly sociable; and, finally, Hume must also be counted among them for he refers to himself as "sociable," adding, however, "though he lives in solitude": he shared his solitude, however, for the most part with good friends and must therefore not be taken quite literally. The shyness which he often displayed was also not so great as to form a serious social impediment.

A large number of thinkers had, on the contrary, a well-defined tendency to a retired life, which evinced itself in many cases in the restriction of their social life to a minimum and in others led to temporary or even permanent seclusion. Locke, who was trained in social matters and who conveyed the impression of a complete man of the world, says of himself that he was by temperament shy of his fellows and therefore made few acquaintances. His rule was "*bene vixit bene qui latuit.*" Mill speaks of his natural tendency to restrict his intercourse to a small circle. "General society," he adds,[1] "as now carried on in England is so insipid an affair, even to the persons who make it what it is, that it is kept up for any reason rather than the pleasure it affords." Spencer, though not otherwise at all diffident in social matters,

[1] Mill, p. 227.

avoided all official functions after he had reached the forties, the only gatherings which he continued to attend being the *soirées* of the Royal Academy.

If these Englishmen's tendency to solitude merely adds a tinge of reserve, a certain ring of self-sufficiency, to lives which were after all reasonably sociable, we find it much more strongly accentuated in a number of Continental thinkers. St Augustine lived for many years alone with his son and a few friends on his estate in Tagaste. Descartes, who came of noble family, enjoying good relations with the court, and was an excellent companion, withdrew for the first time at the age of 18 to the solitude of a quiet suburb: at 33 he went to a lonely castle in Holland, and then lived for five years in the closest seclusion in Amsterdam. Spinoza is the true type of lonely thinker and he had but few friends, from whom he was separated for years. He avoided any other contact with his fellows as far as he possibly could. Greiffenkrantz says[1] of him: "He was always lonely and, as it were, buried alive in his study." Malebranche passed more than half a century in the Oratory in the deepest solitude. Rousseau fled from the noisy life of the town into the silence of the Hermitage which he left after about two years solely because of his quarrel with Mme d'Epinay; he reiterated his detestation of town life and town company and his love of the quiet pleasures of rural solitude, and he passed nearly his whole life in the country. Fichte, too, had a strong tendency towards retirement. As a young man in Königsberg he avoided all social ties; the only friend who gained his intimacy

[1] K. Fischer, Vol. II, p. 189.

had a struggle to overcome Fichte's resistance. When his presence at the dinner table in an inn attracted attention he ceased to go there. At the age of about 35, Schelling developed a marked tendency towards solitude. "I long more and more to be hidden," he wrote in a letter, "and if it depended upon myself, my name would never be mentioned again."[1] Schopenhauer was a solitary figure even as a young man; he did not seek admission to any family in Berlin or frequent any meeting-place. In Frankfurt he lived like a hermit without a single friend until one or two people who knew his writings approached him. Comte avoided social relationships during the period of his marriage and for some time after it; he devoted the whole of his leisure to work. He says himself that his solitude kept him from connexions which would have been valuable. Only towards the end of his life was he surrounded by a circle of followers. Feuerbach lived for thirty-five years in the country in complete retirement from the world. Stirner as a young man was a member of the "Freie," a club composed of writers, journalists and politicians, but he was silent and retiring, seldom taking part in discussion and making a friend of no one. Indeed, he never had an intimate friend and never associated with any other circle of people; he passed his life with the minimum of social intercourse, if not entirely without any. Mackay says of him that his life was as lonely as his thought. Nietzsche, even as a young professor at Basel, began to avoid evening engagements. Even before he laid down his professorship he found that it suited him well to live

[1] K. Fischer, Vol. VII, p. 169.

alone. Shortly afterwards he wrote,[1] "I cannot associate with human beings," and again,[2] "I cannot express how much good solitude does me." He lived later as a hermit in Sils-Maria in Switzerland. Once when a visitor was announced he became so enraged that he wrote,[3] "If I cannot make sure of being alone, I swear I will leave Europe for five years."

All these men, then, had a distaste, whether transient or lasting, for social life; they had, as Locke expressed it, a ". . . temper always shy . . . of strangers,"[4] or, at least, periods of such shyness in their lives—at all events a trait of character deviating conspicuously from those movements of foregathering and mutual encouragement which actuate ordinary human beings. We must, therefore, agree with v. Gwinner when he writes: "All human geniuses thus seem inevitably to run to excess and thereby become so little fitted for life in this world that the great poets were nearly always unhappy and the great thinkers nearly always misanthropic."[5]

Over and above this, we find in many of them, and in a number of others, a degree of self-assertiveness, of conceit, of aggressiveness—in a word, of unbearableness—which drove their friends away and led them into serious differences with those around them. Plato was by no means innocent of blame for his conflicts with Dionysius the Elder and his son; the immense egotism and obstinacy which characterized him were bound to rouse the opposition of the Tyrants. Bruno, as we have already mentioned, made enemies everywhere through his rude-

[1] Nietzsche, *Briefe* II, p. 417. [2] *Ibid.*, p. 439. [3] *Ibid.*, p. 460.
[4] King (Peter), Lord, *Life of John Locke*, p. 247. [5] v. Gwinner, p. 253.

ness; whilst enjoying English hospitality, he attacked, in his *Cena de la Cenere*, English conditions and the English character so violently as to turn every one into an enemy. At the trial of his benefactor and friend, Essex, Bacon turned upon him pitilessly, although it was a question of life and death, and even after the execution he again came forward in justification of the Queen's action. His morbid suspicions led Rousseau to throw over nearly all his friends; he broke with his benefactress, Mme d'Epinay, and with Diderot because he believed that they had betrayed the secret of his love for Mme d'Houdetot and with Holbach because of Holbach's alleged arrogance towards him, and he made most serious accusations against Hume, who, sincerely sympathetic, had offered him a refuge in England. Fichte everywhere developed highly unedifying relations with his colleagues. He was consequently telling the truth when he wrote to his brother: "I can be on intimate terms with hardly anybody." Schelling was still more aggressive; he came into serious conflict with his colleague Paulus and he broke with Fichte and even with his most intimate friends Hegel and Röschlaub—all for the sake of philosophic differences of opinion. A passage in a book by his faithful friend Windischmann, which displeased him, led him to use the most offensive terms and, in spite of all offers of apology, to force matters to a rupture. Nor was Schopenhauer's treatment of his followers any better. Frauenstädt, who had done the greatest possible service in spreading Schopenhauer's philosophy, he violently denounced in a letter, accusing him of making concessions to materialism and, when Frauenstädt was stung to a reply, did not write him another word for three years. Comte was, even as a child, continually at war with his school teachers and supervisors. He threw over his master and friend St Simon after a few years of collaboration; similarly, he quarrelled with his friends, Eichthal and de Blainville, to whom he owed the greatest gratitude—with the one because he had shown leanings towards the St Simonians, with the other owing to a quite unimportant and moreover unintentional offence. De Blainville had published his *Course of Biology* through the offices of a clergyman who had inserted some derogatory observations about Comte without the knowledge of the author; de Blainville had the passage removed as soon as it was brought to his attention. Comte seemed to be appeased but was unable to refrain from making a bitter reference in his oration at his friend's grave. He offended Mill, who most unselfishly procured him financial support in England, by making quite senseless charges and, finally, he fell foul of his pupil Littré, who had also rendered him material service with energy and success.

Unsociableness is a factor which made many philosophers incapable of social relations even when they wished for them; in the case of many others it was a certain awkwardness or uncouthness which led to the infringement of conventional forms. Socrates, it is true, eagerly sought social relations with his fellowmen for "The men who dwell in the city are my teachers and not the trees, or the country."[1] But he made enemies of these men by trying to convince them that, although they might think themselves wise, they were not. Leibniz, afraid of his

[1] Plato, *Phaedrus*, 230.

clumsiness and his ignorance of the ways of the aristocratic world, did not dare to accept the post of Secretary to the Danish Minister. Fechner says of himself:[1] "Accustomed to intellectual occupation, with little capacity for dealing with people and for social intercourse, capable indeed of nothing but working with a book and a pen in my hand, I soon began to feel all the tortures of deathly boredom." Spencer said outright that his most prominent characteristic was probably his lack of social tact.

To sum up—seven of our thirty philosophers show no particular peculiarity in the matter of social intercourse; of one, Aristotle, we know nothing definite; the remaining twenty-two, however, exhibit the characteristics which we have come to recognize and on the strength of which we may say that most of the great philosophers were diffident in, or unsuited for, social intercourse.

The unsocial character of the great thinkers had already attracted Plato's attention. The philosopher, he found, does not concern himself with clubs, banquets, or revels with girl flute-players, nor has he any notion what his fellows and neighbours are about; his helplessness makes him ridiculous everywhere.[2] Similarly, Schopenhauer observes that "few men indeed of this kind, even though they may have the best of characters, show that intimate and unbounded understanding towards their friends, their family and the community at large, of which many of the others are capable."[3] Spranger also emphasizes that "the true theoretician does not fall within the category of socially-inclined natures."[4]

[1] K. Lasswitz, p. 40. [2] *Theaetetus*, 174-5.
[3] *Aphorismen zur Lebensweisheit. Sämmtliche Werke*, V, p. 359.
[4] p. 118.

I may say here, once for all, that the words "unsuited for a profession," "unsuited to earn money," "unsuited for marriage," and "unsuited for social intercourse," express my meaning in a way which is suitable for the worst cases but is too severe for the milder ones. In the strict sense of the word, a man like Leibniz, who was for years and decades the intimate friend of women of high rank, cannot strictly be called unsuited for social intercourse, even though he was helpless and awkward. This is a characteristic which may express itself in very different degrees and only the final degree of which—the last link in the chain, so to speak—would justify the term "unsuitability," whilst the finer shades would only appear as an impediment to, and a clog upon, action. "Unsuitable" is therefore to be understood here as an *a fortiori* adjective, for which, strictly speaking, the expression "varying from more or less impeded to actually unfit" should be substituted. But in order to avoid using this clumsy phrase let us keep to the above terminology and say: "the philosophers are for the most part either diffident in, or unsuited for, social intercourse."

CHAPTER XII

POLITICS

CAREER and money, love and marriage, together with social intercourse, fill up the greater part of the life of the average man; participation in public life, although by no means rare, is still not so common that a man becomes conspicuous if he abstains from it. In this matter there is no average line of conduct with which we can compare the political behaviour of the philosophers: we will therefore regard it in the first place as an uncorrelated phenomenon,[1] simply because it does, after all, constitute a very important and common human activity.

The results which we have so far obtained enable us to approach this study with a definite question in mind: do the philosophers behave in politics with as much hesitancy and such lack of skill as in other matters? We see at once that of our thirty thinkers very few were capable politicians. The best was, again, undoubtedly Hume who, first as secretary and later as deputy to the British Ambassador in Paris, and finally as Under-Secretary of State, showed much cleverness and attained great success. Far below him stands Bacon who, in spite of having reached the office of Lord Chancellor and occupying for

[1] Correlation will be furnished by the behaviour of other people interested in politics. See p. 104.

thirty-seven years a distinguished position in Parliament, where he was a first-class speaker, had not a very happy touch in his more important political undertakings. Thus, under Elizabeth, he conducted a useless opposition to the government's bill to subsidize a war against Spain and he even advised James I on the one hand to conduct an anti-Spanish foreign policy and on the other to use the proposal for a matrimonial alliance with the Spanish ruling house as a means of pressure to obtain money from Parliament. His acceptance of bribes as a judge was also a piece of folly since he was well aware of the growing opposition to this abuse. Mill must also be mentioned in this connexion; he was a Member of Parliament for three years after having for a long time shewn reluctance to accept that position; he supported schemes of social reform—not without initial success—but he failed to be re-elected after his first session. An earlier enterprise of his, the revival of the English Radical party, was also a failure. And, finally, Locke displayed little energy; the political situation in England disgusted him so much at times that he wanted to emigrate. He refused posts as ambassador at Berlin and Vienna. For a considerable time he was adviser to Shaftesbury; as Trade Commissioner he longed to retire from political life and after a year he proffered his resignation.

Over against these four there stands a phalanx of thinkers who took no part or only a sporadic part in active politics. Socrates could not bring himself to appear in public assemblies; his daemon, his inner warning voice, held him back. Epicurus had a strong dislike for all political activity; and even his philosophy expresses this, for he taught that political activities should be avoided because they lead men away from the paths of wisdom and happiness. St Augustine and Bruno took no part in politics; similarly, Hobbes was not an active politician. Descartes, Spinoza, Malebranche, and Berkeley refrained from mixing in political life, and Rousseau even refused to draft constitutions for Corsica and Poland when asked to do so. He was well aware of his unsuitability for political activities, for he wrote that nature had denied him the talent to be a public man—a man of action. Kant was so shy of intervening in political matters that in spite of his burning interest in the French Revolution he refused the offer of an exchange of letters with the Abbé Siéyès. Regarding Fichte, only the *Reden an die deutsche Nation* need be mentioned, and whilst these represent indeed an attempt to exert political influence, his attitude was for the rest passive. Hegel wrote a few essays on current political subjects but did not have them printed. Schelling displayed no political activity. Herbart wrote: "The thinker must never attempt to influence his age directly,"[1] and he followed his own principle closely. Schopenhauer asserted at 31 that nothing was further from his mind than any tendency to engage in politics and he never abandoned this attitude. Fechner wrote political articles in the year 1848 and also became a civic guard, but apart from that he held himself aloof from politics. Feuerbach, in 1848-49 delivered his "Lectures on the nature of Religion," but never made any other public appearance; he was opposed to the suggestion that he should be elected to Parliament.

[1] Fritzsch, p. 23.

Stirner took not the slightest public part in the political events of 1848. Thus, not even that year of wild happenings was able to shake the four last-named out of their passivity. Spencer only took part in politics once in his life, when he associated himself with the agitation for the extension of the franchise. Hartmann and Nietzsche took no active part whatever in politics. Thus, no fewer than 22 of our 30 philosophers were to all intents and purposes completely inactive politically.

Four remain of whom we cannot make this assertion, but who have the other defect that in their political activities they were far from astute. This may perhaps be denied in the case of Leibniz but it must after all be recognized that all his big political plans broke down. At the age of 23 he proved by mathematics that it was essential to make the Elector Palatine of Neuburg King of Poland, but without success. Three years later he worked out a scheme for the conquest of Egypt by Louis XIV and endeavoured to persuade the King to accept it, in order to turn him from war with Holland and at the same time to rid the German Empire of the Turkish danger. Louis' Secretary of State replied: "I say nothing about the scheme for a Holy War, but you must know that such schemes have gone out of fashion since the days of St Louis." And, indeed, any feeling for fashion at all or for what was in keeping with the spirit of the times was foreign to Leibniz, for all his intelligence; and without such feeling all political plans are doomed in advance to sterility. His opposition to the Peace of Utrecht was also a failure, as were his attempt to persuade Austria to continue her war against France, his efforts, which lasted thirty years, to restore the unity of the Catholic and Protestant churches—when he placed his trust again and again in Louis XIV, the very man who was opposed to such reunion if only for political reasons—and finally, his action in the efforts to secure the union of the Lutheran and Reformed Churches. It must also be borne in mind that his dual ties with Berlin and Hanover aroused mistrust on both sides, with the result that he left Berlin permanently in 1711.

Plato's failures were still more notable. As a youth he made it his aim to devote himself to the service of the State as soon as he should come of age. But the misgovernment of the Thirty filled him with such repugnance that he renounced this aim for ever, so far as Athens was concerned; in Syracuse, however, he made his first experiments in practical politics by attempting to obtain influence over the Tyrant, Dionysius. The attempt came to a bad end, however; Plato was arrested and handed over to the Spartan legate and only the intervention of an admirer saved him from being sold as a slave. This experience deterred him from making any further political experiments for the next twenty years. Then, however, he made a further venture, Dionysius having in the meanwhile been succeeded by his son of the same name. It was unsuccessful. A third, five years later, again brought him into great danger. "Plato," says Windelband, very truly, "was a real political thinker, but no statesman; he was filled with yearning for the realization of great schemes but he was no man of action."[1] Aristotle lost his political influence with Alexander, apparently

[1] p. 29.

because he opposed the King's policy of treating Greeks and Barbarians as equals. Finally, Comte enthusiastically joined the revolutionary movement for democracy in 1848 and published a leaflet which led to the foundation of the Positivist Society. He did not, however, gain any political influence thereby.

What figure, then, do the philosophers cut in active politics? A pitiable one. Only Hume can be praised without reserve; Bacon and Mill though they did good political work experienced numerous set-backs; Locke was successful, it is true, but not very active: to sum up, twenty-two were almost entirely passive and the four last-named were clumsy.

The great philosophers, we must again conclude, were nearly all diffident in politics or unsuited for them. It is therefore extremely doubtful whether the salvation of the world can be brought about by applying Plato's formula and making the philosophers kings.[1] Indeed, Plato knew better himself, for in the *Theaetetus* he portrays with great clarity the unfitness of the philosopher for politics. The philosopher "from his youth knows neither the way to the market nor where the law court, the town hall or any other public building lies."[2] And if he has to speak in public, whether in court or elsewhere, his helplessness and his lack of knowledge of the world are fatal to him.[2] This forms a good illustration of the thesis stated above: the great philosophers were nearly all diffident in politics or unsuited for them.

[1] *Republic*, 473.

[2] Plato, *Theaetetus*, 173.

CHAPTER XIII

SYNOPSIS: THE PHILOSOPHER IN PRACTICAL LIFE

PRACTICAL life—life, as opposed to thought—consists in the pursuit of an occupation, in earning money, in marriage, social intercourse, and political activity. In all these spheres, however, the philosophers are loth to act;[1] in this they seem wise, for when they do act they act for the most part foolishly. Nietzsche says with acuity: "a certain type of man does himself most service by abstaining from action as far as possible."[2] And in all these spheres, again, the philosophers—to follow the expressions which we have used hitherto—are diffident or unsuited; in a word, they are diffident in life or unsuited for it. There is in them a tendency to turn away from life, an ascetic trend; they are, as Schopenhauer says, a kind of natural monks, and they have in addition a remoteness from life, a helplessness, a lack of the "sense of concrete things,"[3] as Spranger expresses it. "The pure percipient of knowledge is helpless when faced with the practical tasks of life."[4]

As I have already emphasized, there lies in these characteristics a divergence from the average man, the

[1] Spencer says of himself: "Thinking was always with me more pleasurable than either reading or doing." (Vol. I, p. 351.)

[2] *Wille zur Macht, Werke*, XV, 1901, § 78.

[3] p. 119.

[4] Spranger, p. 113.

normal, whose characteristic traits are his activity in practical life and his suitability for it. This divergence is a negative variation,[1] a lagging back behind the mean, an inadequate adjustment to external conditions, an unfitness to meet the tasks of life. Nietzsche says: "There is something ailing in the whole type of philosophers as we have known them; they must have developed wrongly in many respects."[2] But in how many? Is there an answer to this question? Is it possible to estimate at once the amount of unsuitability and of divergence from the normal? If I attempt to do this, I will not promise a degree of exactitude which cannot be attained in this field, but I will be content to give the most striking and graphic picture possible of the insufficiency of the great philosophers to meet the demands of life. Let us suppose that a man who is "normal," that is to say, active and fit, in all five divisions of practical life would get five marks and that one is deducted for each division in which our philosophers are "not normal," *i.e.*, inactive or unfit. Then, out of 30:—

No philosopher gets 5 marks.
1 „ „ 4 „
3 philosophers get 3 „
7 „ „ 2 „
7 „ „ 1 mark,

and no less than

12 philosophers get 0 marks.

[1] This is true of the majority of cases, but in periods and places where interest in philosophy is strong it may also be a positive variation. The value attached to these terms is to be understood solely in the biological sense, *e.g.*, as implying lesser or greater ability to make headway in life.

[2] *Werke*, XIII, § 48.

Thus, where thirty "normal" men would score 150 marks, our thirty thinkers only score 34. The remainder, 116, shows, as it were, the degree of unsuitability, which amounts to 3·9 per head, as against 0 in the case of "normal" people.

We must also point out a remarkable peculiarity in the practical behaviour of the philosophers—the variableness of their activity. Their practical activity was, as we have seen, for the most part small, but its low level, instead of remaining constant, was in the case of not a few thinkers subject to variations due partly to periods of greater activity, or of particularly conspicuous inactivity, in their lives and partly to the fact that with the approach of age they grew ever more active or, on the other hand, ever more inactive. We find periods of increased activity exemplified in Plato's three political adventures and we know of periods of reduced practical activity and even of complete inactivity in the lives of Descartes, Rousseau, Comte, Fechner, and Mill, which were due—except in the case of Descartes—to nervous illnesses.

An instance of practical activity which gradually increased is afforded by Hume who was until 50 a scholar only, but then became a practical politician. But we find much more frequently the opposite development, in which the normal or at all events the moderate activity displayed in youth suddenly or gradually falls off. St Augustine furnishes an example of sudden falling-off in sexual life, Descartes in professional life. The diminution of practical activity was gradual in Schelling, Spencer and Nietzsche.

We may conclude that :—

1. The great philosophers were inactive in, and unsuited for, practical life—in a word, they displayed insufficiency ;

2. The amount of practical activity is subject to variation in the course of a lifetime.

CHAPTER XIV

CONDITIONS OF NORMAL BEHAVIOUR IN PRACTICAL LIFE

THE result to which our biographical study has led us is that the practical insufficiency of the philosophers is a fact of decisive importance for their fortunes. Can we explain this fact ? Can we say why these keen thinkers were so hesitant to act, why these successful theoreticians were such unsuccessful practicians ? We have studied the behaviour of the philosopher in his profession, his money matters, his marriage, and his social relations, as opposed to normal behaviour—" normal " being used merely in the sense of " most general " or " usual " behaviour. We then found that the type comprising the philosopher, with his lack of activity and his unsuitability for practical life, was in this respect an inferior variation as compared with " normal," and we extended the notion of " normal " in our further considerations to include its other characteristics of biological serviceableness, of appropriateness, of utility in the struggle for existence.

If then we wish to understand how this inferior variation comes into existence, we shall do better to begin by considering what is normal and by observing what are the conditions of activity and fitness, in other words of normal behaviour, in practical life. All action is ultimately traceable to impulses, without which the psycho-physical apparatus would be like an engine without steam.[1] What are the impulses? Firstly hunger, thirst, or the opposite impulse, disgust; then fatigue, in so far as it includes the impulses to lie down, to close the eyes and to innervate the flexor muscles; the sex-impulse, shame, jealousy, the impulse towards self-decoration or vanity, love of children, pugnacity, the impulse to escape, or fear, the herd instinct and the impulse to help, or sympathy, the instincts of leadership and of subordination and the desire for knowledge, or curiosity. To these we must add the impulses connected with the numerous and varied feelings of liking and dislike, such as the instinct to sniff a pleasant odour and to avoid an unpleasant one, to consume things, *e.g.*, cigars, the consumption of which gives pleasure, when in pain to rub the spot or run about blind. The first-named, the instincts, characterized by their inheritability, the fact that they were originally present to an equal extent in all individuals of the same kind, their appropriateness to the end they serve and their adaptability, are distinguished, by the definite character of the actions to which they give rise, from the pathematic[2] impulses, which are associated with a more generalized tendency towards movement, *i.e.*, with unrest—although in their case, it is true, the painful part receives special attention. We need only compare, for example, the highly specialized actions which serve to satisfy hunger

[1] Kretschmer, p. 111.

[2] [" *Pathematic* "—This word, which has fallen a little into disuse, affords so exact a rendering of "*gefühlsbetont*"—" fraught with pleasure or displeasure "—that I make no excuse for reviving it in the sense in which Jeremy Bentham (cf. *Psyche*, July 1928, p. 17) and others (*v.* OED) have used it.—*Trs.*]

or the sex-impulse with the wild behaviour of a person suffering from severe toothache, or contrast the actions of a dog or small child at liberty with their attempts to escape if shut up in a cage.

Three points call, however, for attention in making this distinction: firstly, the instincts and pathematic impulses merge into one another after numerous intermediate stages have been passed, as is evidenced by the impulses derived from smells and tastes; secondly, it is only a question of a greater or lesser degree of definiteness or specialization, even in the case of the characteristic instances of both groups; and thirdly, pathematic movements are only indefinite and generalized at the commencement of the individual development and soon become definite and specialized as the result of experience.

The instincts, properly so-called, and the pathematic impulses have, however, a common psychophysical structure. We find in the first place a sensation: in hunger an empty sensation in the stomach, in fatigue a heaviness of the muscles, in appetite a watering of the mouth—let us call it an initial sensation. These sensations are pathematic, conveying dissatisfaction not only in the case of hunger, fatigue, sex-excitement, and pity but also in the case of impulses which have their roots in pleasurable experiences, *e.g.*, the taste impulses or those to smoke or take morphia. We often read that where an impulse has never been satisfied, the experience is confined to the initial sensation and the pathematic content. Such is, however, not the case, for even where satisfaction has never been experienced the sex-impulse, for instance, is accompanied by a kind of unrest—that is, by sensations in the body muscles and by a variety of movements. This unrest, occurring in greater or lesser degree, is thus the third factor in every experience of impulse. Finally, it also embodies the ideas connected with the satisfaction of the impulse and the actions and objects necessary to it; these again convey feelings—this time of a pleasurable nature—which, together with the displeasurable character of the initial sensations, bring about the peculiarly mixed feelings connected with the experience of the impulse. Accordingly, the impulse may be shortly defined as a dispositive complex of movements or actions activated by a sensation fraught with displeasure.

Only in the lower animals do the impulses remain as they were inherited, so that all their developments throughout life are conditioned solely by the cropping up of fresh inherited instincts. In all beings which are in any way capable of learning, the impulses begin to develop their action under the influence of experience.

The causes of this development are, firstly, that impulses frequently cannot be satisfied directly for reasons lying outside themselves, *e.g.*, hunger, the sex-impulse and appetite, and secondly, that impulses are often repressed by counter-impulses, *e.g.*, pugnacity by fear and the sex-impulse by shame. The first factor leads to the impulse's being diverted from the end to the means; a person who is annoyed by flies in his room experiences in the first place an impulse to drive them off. This impulse will be diverted to a variety of mediative actions which seem to him appropriate, *e.g.*, killing flies, hanging up fly-papers, removing food remains, etc. In the same way the sex-impulse is diverted into mediative actions such as conversing, going for walks and making presents, and hunger into the preparation of food or working for daily bread. The majority of our actions are impulse-activities of this indirect kind.

The diversion of impulses occurs not only from end to means but also from one set of actions and objects to a similar set—particularly under the influence of the second factor, inhibition. Thus the impulse to play chess is to be explained as a combative impulse which, diverted from its original methods and aims by the inhibitive action of fear, has sought expression in this analogous activity; the impulse to keep and to be kind to animals is a diverted love of children. All games are substituted activities of this kind.

One aspect of this diversion of impulses calls for our greatest attention: it may happen that an action or an object is not solely the means of satisfying one impulse but is appropriate to the satisfaction of several; thus clothing not only protects from cold but also serves the sense of shame and vanity, and money is a universal means for the satisfaction of nearly all impulses. In such cases of a convergence of impulses, compounds are formed—impulses of a higher order, as it were—which assume a single and specialized character, as for instance the interest in clothes, in money, or in philosophy, the highly complex nature of which we have already analysed.

In addition to diversion and convergence, impulses may develop in a third manner: impulse and counter-impulse do not generally cancel out but give rise in turn to special products, impulse resultants, one of which we have just noted in the form of interest in chess; others, similarly constituted, are to be sought in the interest in ridicule and satire. Compounded of the sex-impulse on the one hand and the sense of shame together with other inhibitions on the other, is the impulse to dance.

We have referred to indirect impulses, compounded impulses and impulse resultants as interests and it is these interests which lead directly to practical action, and indeed to every form of activity. Hence, normal practical behaviour is conditional upon normal practical interests. But what are normal interests?

First of all, interests properly so called, *i.e.*, higher developments of the impulses, must be present; the primitive impulses are not enough. Where they have not developed into a professional, pecuniary, matrimonial or social interest, as for example in the case of mental defectives, no normal practical behaviour will ensue. The existence of practical interests in turn presupposes that no important individual basic impulse—*e.g.*, the sex-impulse, the herd instinct or vanity—is lacking, for this would result in the absence or a diminution of the interests arising out of them. Furthermore, there must be present a certain degree of intelligence, without which no diversion of impulses, and, in turn, no convergence and no production of resultants is possible.

Secondly, the interests, or rather the impulses upon which they are based, must have a certain intensity. If this is insufficient, as with very phlegmatic temperaments, activity and efficiency will also suffer.

Thirdly, the interests must harmonize; that is to say, no one of them must so predominate as to draw a disproportionate share of the total energy of the individual to itself; if sex interest, money interest or the interest in collecting things dominates the others, normal practical behaviour is, again, impossible.

The presence of the practical interests, a certain intensity on their part, and harmony between them, are therefore essential to normal practical behaviour.

CHAPTER XV

IS UNSUITABILITY FOR PRACTICAL LIFE DUE TO THE ABSENCE OR WEAKNESS OF INTERESTS ?

We have already asked where the cause of the philosophers' unsuitability for practical life is to be sought. Now that we have seen what the conditions of normal practical behaviour are we may put this question in a more precise form : which of these conditions do the philosophers fail to fulfil ? Are they people without practical interests, have they practical interests but in an insufficiently intense form, or are the practical interests, though sufficiently intense, eclipsed by another interest ?

If we were to judge by our first impression of the life histories of the great thinkers, we might be inclined to answer all three questions in the affirmative. The philosophers seem to pass high over the petty interests of everyday life, their gaze directed towards lofty goals, untouched and undisturbed by the strife of mankind, untrammelled by professional cares, above the pursuit of money, unclaimed by love, marriage or society, free of the political whirlpool—is not that life without practical interests ? Do not those of them who go down to the stony places where men's life-work is performed stumble over every rock of professional difficulty, fall into every pit of economic ruin and get caught in every noose of political intrigue? And do they not thereby prove how small their practical interests are? Finally, the complete predominance of one interest, the philosophical, over all others is, after all, what makes the philosopher: can it be doubted that the reason why Thales fell into the brook was that his gaze was directed to the skies?

Yes, all this may be doubted; indeed it is better to doubt it and, refusing to trust to superficial impressions, to examine the lives of the great thinkers thoroughly, under the microscope as it were, in order to ascertain which of these possibilities has been realized.

Let us, then, take the hypothesis of a lack of practical interests and, at the same time, the other hypothesis, which cannot in practice be separated from it—that of weakness of interest, which we find mentioned in Plato's *Republic* in the following words: "When a person's desires set strongly in one direction, they run with corresponding feebleness in every other channel, like a stream whose waters have been diverted into another bed."[1] These hypotheses might explain the passivity of the philosophers and their unsuitability for practical life, since when we have little or no interest in a thing, we do not spend much time on it, or, if we do, it is usually without achieving much. But do they fit in with the facts? Do they give us a *vera causa?* Have the philosophers really no practical interests?

We will not speak of professional interests; we know too little of them. Of pecuniary interests we also know little, but that little is of importance: Socrates, Epicurus, Descartes, Spinoza, Rousseau, Feuerbach, and Spencer

[1] 485.

showed no inclination to earn money; they must have been completely lacking in pecuniary interest. In Bacon, Leibniz, and Schopenhauer this interest was, however, very active; yet, as we have seen, they also displayed certain signs of inaptitude although to a slight extent.

Of the unmarried philosophers, again, there is every reason for assuming that Plato and Malebranche had no interest in matrimony. Of Epicurus and Hobbes, we know nothing for certain. Bruno, Leibniz, and Hume had at all events a certain interest in women; Descartes had a liaison which lasted for several years. But all the remainder, seven in number, definitely had matrimonial plans. St Augustine, after he had left the woman who had been his companion for many years, was impatient to marry. Locke speaks of his cousin as the beloved being with whom he wished to share his life. Spinoza intended to marry the daughter of his teacher, van den Ende. Kant was twice on the point of proposing marriage. It was only after a severe inward struggle that Schopenhauer gave up the plans to marry which he had entertained for many years. Spencer, in the course of weighing the advantages and disadvantages of emigrating to New Zealand, gave most marks, among the "pros" to the possibility of marriage. "The relative values assigned," he says, "make it clear that a state of celibacy was far from being my ideal."[1] Nietzsche, in his letters, reverts time after time to his matrimonial plans; in one letter he even passes his female acquaintances in review in order to select a suitable mate. These men, consequently, had a quite definite interest in marriage, some of them even

[1] Vol. I, pp. 370-1.

an intensive and lasting one. Yet they did not marry. Here then, still more clearly than in the monetary sphere, the fact stands out that insufficiency is based not on the absence or even the weakness of the interest concerned but exists in spite of the presence of an active interest.

Nor can the explanation of social inaptitude be sought in a complete lack of the interest concerned. It is true that many of the great thinkers led secluded lives, but none of them went out into the desert in order to make certain of avoiding all contact with his fellows: none of them lived entirely without friends or acquaintances, like an Indian ascetic. We must therefore presuppose that they had a certain interest in social intercourse with others. It may be that in the case of many—Descartes, Malebranche, Spinoza, Fechner, and Feuerbach—it was very slight; we do not know for certain. In others, however—*e.g.*, Epicurus, Hobbes, Hume, Kant, Hegel, and Hartmann—it was highly developed, as we have seen; these men, moreover, lived social lives. It is remarkable, too, that Socrates, though not free from signs of social inaptitude, showed great interest in social intercourse; it is still more remarkable that this interest was exceptionally strong in the three thinkers who were the most lonely and socially the least developed, so that the outbreaks to which it occasionally gave rise are particularly impressive. Thus Rousseau wrote to the Maréchale de Luxembourg that he had spent his life in a vain quest for lasting friendships. And in his *Rêveries du Promeneur Solitaire*, he says of himself: "the most sociable and friendly of men was proscribed by unanimous agreement. In the refinement of their hatred they sought for the torment which would wound my sensitive soul most cruelly and they violently broke all the liens which united me to them."[1] Schopenhauer writes, similarly, that he felt terribly lonely throughout his life and always sighed from his heart: "Oh! let me find a human being!" In vain. And Nietzsche wrote: "There are good reasons for the absence of the people who belong to me and it would be ridiculous for a philosopher to expect it otherwise. Still, my longing for some extraordinary piece of luck will not die; it is terrible to be so alone."[2] And again: "Seven years of solitude have passed; at heart I am by no means fitted for it and now that I can no longer see how I may avoid it I feel nearly every week so sudden a disgust for life that it makes me ill."[3] Here then, we again have on the one hand cases in which social inaptitude is, at all events potentially, traceable to the slightness of the social interest, and on the other hand cases in which it is incontestable that symptoms of insufficiency, even of a high degree, may be present at the same time as strong and permanent interest.

There remain politics. Here again we have found the philosophers inactive and inefficient and we are the more inclined to ascribe this deficiency back to a lack of political interests in that in political respects the philosophers do not, as in the rest of their practical lives, differ from the ordinary run of men, whose political passivity and inefficiency is undoubtedly due to political indifference. But this assumption must be corrected in

[1] *Ière Promenade*, p. 195.
[2] *Briefe*, II, p. 629.
[3] *Briefe*, II, p. 650.

view of the actual facts which are that, of the twenty-two philosophers who abstained or practically abstained from active politics, no fewer than fifteen wrote on political problems—namely Epicurus, Hobbes, Spinoza, Berkeley, Rousseau, Kant, Fichte, Hegel, Schelling, Herbart, Schopenhauer, Stirner, Spencer, Hartmann, and Nietzsche. Socrates was also particularly fond of introducing politics into his conversations. This deep and even fundamental, though theoretical, concern with politics proves how active was the political interest of these men despite their absolutely passive attitude towards political life. Consequently, only the remaining six—St Augustine, Bruno, Descartes, Malebranche, Fechner, and Feuerbach —who touched upon political themes either very lightly or not at all, may be accounted politically uninterested. Again, Plato, Aristotle, Leibniz, and Comte, who although not passive were less adroit in active politics, wrote voluminous, valuable, and, in fact, epoch-making political works, so that here again there can be no question of tracing their political inaptitude to a lack of political interest. With Plato, in particular, we know that political interest was a veritable passion, for which he endeavoured to find an outlet at the Court of Syracuse since he was unable to gratify it at home. Leibniz, again, refused the post of professor at Altdorf out of longing to take part in political life, and in the revolution of 1848 Comte at once attempted to put his political ideas into practice. All this completely proves that the majority of the great philosophers took a lively interest in politics, but that this interest led either to inadequate action or, more often, to none at all, being translated into thinking or political philosophizing alone. Spencer recognized this clearly; he wrote, of a political enterprise: "If I had duly borne in mind the general principle of the specialization of functions in mind at that time, I should have seen that my function was to think rather than to act. I should never have entertained the intention here indicated."[1] The political inaptitude of the philosophers is, accordingly, something quite different from that of the ordinary man, for whilst the latter is in general based upon or accompanied by political indifference, in the philosopher it usually asserts itself in spite of a lively political interest. From this we may see that the philosophers diverge from the normal not only in professional and money matters, in marriage and in social life, but also in politics. In establishing a comparison, however, we must not cite those normal people who may perhaps be politically as inactive as the majority of philosophers, but normal people interested in politics, who would for the most part demonstrate their interest by active participation in political life—just what the great majority of the philosophers fail to do.

What is the reason for the unsuitability of the philosophers for practical life? This question is in the main still unanswered. In the field of professional life it may be due to lack of interest—we do not know; in money matters it certainly is due to this in a number of cases; but in other cases interest is present and in the questions of marriage, social intercourse, and politics we have given a considerable number of examples in which typical

[1] Vol. II, p. 330.

symptoms of unsuitability for practical life are found side by side with a lively practical interest.

In so doing we have destroyed one suggestion which might have been put forward as explaining a remoter cause of practical inadequacy, namely the absence of certain instincts, *e.g.*, the sex impulse or the social instinct. Men who lack these instincts must also lack the interests which grow out of them, such as matrimonial or social interest, or at all events these interests must be very slight, if only because they can then be derived from subsidiary sources alone. But we have seen that in numerous cases they are not slight and we may venture to assert by analogy that they will not be slight in many other cases where we cannot bring actual proof.

Thus we may sum up as follows: the unsuitability of the philosophers for practical life is due in a number of cases to the absence or the weakness of practical interests; in many other cases, probably the majority, it exists side by side with lively practical interests.

CHAPTER XVI

THE PHILOSOPHERS AS MEN WITH STRONG IMPULSES

THE assumption that the unsuitability of the philosophers for practical life is due to weakness of practical interest is not conclusive, as we have seen, and is in many cases even false, for the majority, or at all events a considerable number, of our thinkers had on the contrary very strong practical interests. From this fact we may draw a valuable conclusion regarding the part played by impulse in the life of the philosophers, for if the interests are strong, their components, the impulses, must also have been of considerable intensity.

What exactly do we mean by the intensity of an impulse? In the first place, we feel the intensity of thirst, love-longing or fear directly; their intensity constitutes what is importunate, assertive, obsessing and devastating in them, and is certainly a real characteristic of the experience. Secondly, we estimate the intensity of an impulse by its effects, both by the gestures giving it expression and by the actions to which it gives rise: thus we call an impulse, such as anger, intense when the gestures expressing it, including the words spoken, are violent, when the actions cover a considerable period of time or are carried through in the face of considerable opposition—when, in short, they are profuse or energetic.

The predisposition to experience impulses intensely—recognizable either subjectively or through expressive gestures—we call passionateness.

The philosophers showed little activity in practical life and we must not expect profuse or energetic action of them ; the intensity of their impulses will in consequence be expressed mainly in their subjective experiences, their gestures, and their speech. What do we know of these ?

There is a well-known story of Phaedon's to the effect that an Oriental physiognomist said that he read passionate sensuality in the face of Socrates. Alcibiades is reported to have laughed aloud at this but Socrates admitted that the man was right ; it was indeed within him but he had overcome it through the λόγος. We have no reason to doubt the truth of this self-revelation ; indeed, Socrates is credited in other quarters with a warm and strongly sensuous temperament.[1]

Nor can we avoid regarding Plato as a man with powerful impulses. His letters brim over with wrath against Dionysius, his *Laws* contain the most spirited attacks on the atheists, and the love that inspired the *Banquet* must have been indeed a passionate one. St Augustine continually complains of the lust and pride that raged within him. He is never tired of describing the bitter torments of carnal desire and his continual struggle with the currents of voluptuousness which carry him helplessly along. This, added to the heat of his religious ardour, betokens the greatest passion, the most intense impulse of which any human being is capable.

Bruno was also a man full of passionate unrest with

[1] Wilamowitz, p. 112, footnote 3.

an impulsive and aggressive nature. We have already seen how his violence brought him enemies everywhere and how, in particular, he harmed himself by his savage attack on England in *La Cena de le Cenere*. Flaming enthusiasm for knowledge, for the new science, leaps from the pages of his works: "*nam tangente Deo fervidus ignis eris* (for if God touch thee, thou wilt be a flame of fire)." We learn without surprise that tradition ascribes to him great vividness in the use of language.

Hobbes is described as a man of irritable character with eyes which became so animated "that a living coal of fire seemed to shine in them"; [1] he was, in addition, argumentative and intolerant—obstinate and unyielding in defence of his own opinions.

Locke, also, was capable of developing considerable violence in discussion and was easily carried away by anger; he said of himself that he had a warm temperament and this is borne out by the warmth of many of his letters.

We should form a false judgment of Spinoza were we to draw from his quiet life, his invariable friendliness, and his self-control the conclusion that he possessed a phlegmatic temperament, *i.e.*, that his impulses were not intense. It is on the face of things very unlikely that a man who spent so much thought upon the passions and their control should have had none himself, but Colerus definitely reports that Spinoza, when he became angry, often got up and walked away "for fear that his passions might get the upper hand." [2] The murder of de Witt so infuriated him that he wanted to put up a

[1] Tönnies, p. 53.

[2] Gebhardt, p. 70.

notice inscribed "*ultimi barbarorum*" at the place where it occurred and he was only deterred from this action—which might easily have cost him his life—by the fact that his landlord locked up the house.

Rousseau, again, was one of the most passionate of the philosophers; he stands in this respect on the level of St Augustine and Bruno. He describes himself as having a fiery temperament and fierce impetuous passions; he was the prey of devouring sensuality which turned desire into torment and made the anticipation of pleasure far surpass its realization. The fear motive also reached great intensity in him; a cruel imagination, always fearing the worst, tormented him with its pictures of terror. The portrait would be incomplete if anger were left out of it; his temper was so uncontrollable that the epoch-making writer on education was impossible as a teacher.

Fichte's impulsive nature is eloquently expressed in his *Reden an die deutsche Nation*. But not only there; he was one of the very few philosophers who were also capable of being energetic, even inflexible, in action: on account of his well-known hard-headedness the Senate of the University of Berlin, which was at the time engaged in a dispute with the ministry, elected him as rector.

Schelling was above all things a passionate controversialist: when attacked, he was capable of flying into a "frenzy of rage," as he himself called it, and exceeding all bounds.

In this respect he closely resembled Schopenhauer whose polemics against Fichte, Schelling, and particularly Hegel, ended in orgies of abuse: but even apart from scientific quarrels, Schopenhauer had an extremely violent and irritable nature. A delay in printing his work led him to write to his publisher in such offensive terms that the latter broke off further correspondence. It is also well known that in an ungovernable fit of temper he threw an elderly lady downstairs, thus incurring a financial obligation which severely taxed his resources thereafter. He was also uncontrollably sensual. At eighteen he gave expression to the torments which this sensuality caused him in touching verse, and it accompanied him throughout life. If we consider, in addition, the burning ambition which consumed him and made his slowness in attaining to fame so intolerable, and, finally, if we take into account the tormenting fears which frequently beset him without any reason, we may form an idea of the intensity of this man's impulses, which will enable us to understand why he regarded will—blind, unconscious will—as the essence and purport of the world. Only a person consumed by passions could conceive of deliverance from will as the purpose of life.

Comte was by no means so devoid of feeling as might be supposed from the fact that his life was devoted exclusively to his work. He took such a lively interest in the achievements of his pupils that his feelings, as he said, would have led him to tears had he not kept himself well in check. He was also inclined to outbreaks of temper; in his dedication to Clotilde de Vaux he expresses his thanks that she held him back from useless explosions. He characterizes his feeling for her as a deep passion which ploughed up and fructified his whole being.

Nothing that we know of Stirner's life tells us of any particular intensity of impulse, but at times such blinding flashes of passion escape from his works as only a man of mighty impulses could beget.

Finally, Nietzsche forms the last link in the chain of St Augustine, Bruno, Rousseau, and Schopenhauer—and certainly one of its strongest links—for such passion and such volcanic fire as inspires *Zarathustra*, the *Antichrist*, and many of his poems, can seldom have been attained before, and were certainly never surpassed. "Burning with my own thoughts" is the astounding expression which Nietzsche himself finds for the condition in which these works were created.

The assumption that the impulses of the great philosophers must have been of considerable intensity is thus confirmed in respect of half of them. Why not all? Because self-observation and reports on the temperament of the great thinkers are rare and because philosophic works are to a great extent unsuited by their very nature to express passion; moreover, the usual outlet for powerful impulses, continuous and energetic action, is, as we have seen, not to be found in the philosophers. Nevertheless, we shall soon be able to bring complete proof of the accuracy of our assumption. So far, we have established that a large number of the great thinkers were men whose intensity of impulse was considerable.

The philosophers were unsuited for the practical tasks of life; so much we have already seen: we may now add that the lives of many of them were characterized by intensity of impulse. Putting the two facts together we may say that a considerable number of the great thinkers were men of great intensity of impulse but were diffident and inapt in respect of the normal outlet for impulse, action. Each and all of them could say with Faust: "The God in my bosom can stir the deep springs of my soul; but even He who is enthroned above all my own powers cannot move me to deeds."

If, however, this god cannot impel to deeds, if the impulses, for all their intensity, do not lead to action, what do they do? What happens to the psychophysical energy which is stored up in them? An impulse gets under way, initiates a happening, or—as Avenarius expressed it—commences a vital series: what comes next? And how does it end? This question need not cause us any difficulty for we have already answered it in our consideration of the characteristics of philosophic thought; we saw that the life-impulses, instead of ending, as they otherwise would, in practical activity, unite in special circumstances with the desire for knowledge and thus beget philosophic interest and philosophic activity. And when they do this to a considerable extent, when, so to speak, a large quantity of the impulses is united with the desire for knowledge, the latter is on the one hand greatly increased and intensified and on the other qualitatively changed in a characteristic manner—namely, by diversion into a study of those problems which chiefly affect human beings because they deal with the objects of their impulses, that is, with the things that are the final aim of their life-efforts. In a word, the desire for knowledge becomes an intense philosophical interest and the man becomes a philosopher. The god who cannot impel to deeds is content to impel to philosophizing; the active man-god becomes an inactive philosopher-god, an Aristotelian god whose activity consists of thinking only. The life-impulses and interests which are intended to find an outlet in action and would otherwise be directed into the paths of profession, gain, love, marriage, social intercourse and politics, find their outlet in thought, and, instead of marrying, Spinoza writes his thesis on love and jealousy, Schopenhauer his study of women, and Nietzsche his chapter on children and marriage; instead of seeking the company of friends, Schopenhauer and Nietzsche set out to prove that loneliness is the philosopher's lot; instead of taking part in politics Plato and Aristotle, Hobbes and Spinoza, Fichte and Hegel expound the basis of the State. Thinking becomes a substitute for living, philosophizing for doing; the practical interests are taken up and satisfied with philosophizing; philosophy becomes an outlet for impulse.[1] If this is really so, and if the structure of the philosopher's thoughts is exactly the same expression of his impulses as is the normal person's behaviour in practical life, we have found a new factor on which to base our conclusions as to the intensity of human impulses; in both actions and thoughts the factors of profuseness and energy must be our basis in assuming special intensity for the impulses in the background. "Great thoughts come from the heart," said Vauvenargues. And Riehl expressed the same idea when he wrote: "All great things—and the great philosophies are among them—come from the heart and from great passion."[2] All our great thinkers, however, created profound and comprehensive systems of thought by the

[1] Cf. Müller-Freienfels, p. 51.

[2] *Nietzsche*, p. 11.

most persistent effort of mind—a proof that they were all men of strong impulse. "All men of real genius have strong passions," said Shenstone.

Our assumption as to the impulses of the philosophers is thus completely confirmed. All great philosophers, we conclude, are men of great intensity of impulse.

CHAPTER XVII

IS THE PREDOMINANCE OF THE PHILOSOPHIC INTEREST THE CAUSE OF UNSUITABLENESS FOR PRACTICAL LIFE ?

As possible causes of unsuitableness for practical life, we have in the foregoing pages given consideration to deficiency of interests, weakness of interests and disharmony of interests. In many cases, however, there is no absence or weakness of practical interests and there remains only disharmony, *i.e.*, the domination of one interest over all the others. And indeed, if in the case of the Don Juan, the miser, the gambler, collector, or politician, the excess of one interest leads to the serious neglect of other concerns of life, must not the predominance of the speculative interest have the same effect upon the philosopher ?

This hypothesis is a very plausible one ; it appears to furnish a *vera causa*, a really existing fact as the cause of the inability to conduct practical affairs, and one which can be established not only in certain cases but in all, for the predominance of the philosophic interest is to all appearance an unfailing characteristic of the philosophers. Moreover, this hypothesis furnishes an excellent explanation of what it is meant to explain : incessant preoccupation with theory, it would say, takes up so much of the philosopher's time and energy that he does not succeed in learning the lines on which practical life is conducted and, even if he had thoroughly mastered them, the fact that his attention was continually distracted and that he lacked time and energy for practical things would bring about failures, and these failures would in turn lead to a dislike for practical action. A possible difficulty might lie in explaining unsociableness which we have recognized as one of the factors of unsuitableness for practical life, but it would probably be ascribed to the extensive and continuous absorption of the interests in theoretical subjects; a man to whom this happened would find great difficulty in fitting himself into his surroundings; would often misunderstand and be misunderstood by those about him; would frequently find them and their alien concerns disturbing; and finally, if his helplessness and ignorance of practical matters were frequently exploited to his disadvantage, would become reserved and mistrustful. Thus conflicts might easily arise and would indeed be sure to do so where, as is the case with many great thinkers, they were fostered by the presence of a passionate temperament. The varying degrees of inaptitude exhibited by different thinkers and the changes which it underwent throughout their lives would still remain to be explained. In order to do this we should be obliged to assume that whilst the philosophic interest predominated over the others in all the great thinkers, it predominated in varying degrees and with changes of intensity during the life of one and the same man—an assumption which is made *ad hoc* and one for which we have no other basis. Though this may tell against the predominance hypothesis we can, however, find a point in its favour: we have seen that the incapacity of the philosophers in money matters really corresponds to a lack of interest in earning money—indeed to a lack of interest in money altogether. This absence or deficiency of pecuniary interest need not, however, be regarded as a conclusive factor, for pecuniary interest grows gradually in the course of a lifetime through the extension and transfer of the other interests to money, because it constantly proves to be the means of realizing them. If, however, the interest in other things is from the beginning overwhelmed by the philosophic interest and prevented from asserting itself, the result is an interference with the development of the impulses, and the pecuniary interest is developed only partially or not at all.

A hypothesis appealing so directly by its analogies and appearing, in addition, to deal with facts and offer a valuable explanation has naturally not been without its champions. Even Plato makes use of it. Socrates in the *Phaedrus* calls himself a morbidly talkative fellow who would always drop the task in hand in order to listen to a philosophic conversation. Ostwald says of Comte: "The immense concentration upon the labour of thinking which was necessary to the completion of his almost superhuman work robbed him of the greater part of those qualities which cause a person to appear agreeable and attractive in the eyes of others."[1] Gaupp wrote of Spencer: "He analyses everything and tries to explain everything rationally. This purely philosophic turn of mind tends by its very predominance to wither the

[1] p. 72.

other sides of his life."[1] Spranger says: "The other sides of life must necessarily suffer when the value of knowledge is placed above all other values."[2]

This would seem to give an answer to the question as to the origin of the unsuitableness of the great thinkers for practical life, which would thus seem to lie in a disharmony of interests caused by hypertrophy—the overwhelming intensity of the philosophic interest as compared with the practical interests.

Nevertheless, the predominance hypothesis is open to a grave objection. Its basic assumption is the overwhelming and overpowering intensity of the philosophic interest in the great thinkers, as compared with the practical interests. But we have seen that the latter, at all events the erotic, social and political interests, were sometimes very strong in the philosophers—indeed more intense than in the normal man. Yet the lives of the philosophers were dominated not by the practical actions ensuing from these interests but by the thinking which arose from philosophic interest: from this, our hypothesis deduces that, however intense the practical interests were, the philosophic interest was more so. But is this deduction conclusive?

If a man abandons former homosexual relations and marries, are we to draw the conclusion that his heterosexual interest is the greater one? Perhaps; but perhaps, also, he is merely afraid of blackmail or of criminal proceedings and is thereby prevented from giving an outlet to a homosexual impulse which is, in point of fact, the stronger one. Or when Schopenhauer, true to a promise

[1] p. 43. [2] p. 112.

made to his father, gave up his academic career to spend two years in business, did this happen because business interest outweighed interest in learning or because only his dislike of breaking his word kept him from following his far greater interest in the pursuit of knowledge? It is clear that when a person chooses between two lines of conduct the reason may be either that his interest in one of them is the greater or equally that he is afraid or ashamed—*i.e.*, he hesitates—to choose the other. We must also bear in mind the possibility that the philosophers did not reject action and choose thinking because their interest in thinking was greater than their interest in action but because a fear, a hesitation—an impediment of some kind—held them back from action. But this possibility shatters the foundations of the predominance hypothesis, for the predominance of the philosophic interests over the practical ones, which seemed to us just now so certain, is at all events not a fact established by observation but a mere conclusion from the observation that thinking dominates in the lives of the philosophers. It is, however, an uncertain conclusion, for a second possibility exists—that of the inhibition of the practical interests.

To sum up: the hypothesis that the cause of unsuitableness for practical life lies in the predominant intensity of the philosophic interest rests on an uncertain basis, since the fact that thinking prevails in the life of the philosophers can be explained not only by the greater intensity of their philosophic interest but also by the inhibition of their practical interests.

CHAPTER XVIII

A PROVISIONAL STATEMENT OF THE HYPOTHESIS OF INHIBITION

THE hypothesis of predominance, as we have seen, has a competitor whose possibilities we touched upon in an earlier chapter in speaking of the psychology of philosophic thought and of the impulses to action which merge to form philosophic interest. We then found ourselves faced by the question why these impulses to action did not end in action but were forced into the outlet of thought instead. "The reason," we said, "can only lie in the men who behave thus. . . . The theoretical philosopher must be a man who has something in him which prevents him from action."[1] And again, in dealing with the psychology of practical philosophy, we recognized that both inhibitive and incentive ideals were consequences of an impediment to action. "The practical philosopher, too," we conjectured, "must be a man who has something in him which prevents him from action."[2]

These conjectures, with which we concluded our earlier considerations, now derive fresh force; they serve as a new starting point and as a groundwork for the hypothesis which we are now to test. What is this groundwork? The unsuitableness of the philosophers for practical life is

[1] p. 35-6. [2] p. 42.

not a consequence of the predominance of philosophic over practical interests; it is derived, on the contrary, from a different kind of hindrance to these practical interests—a barrier in the way of the outlet which they seek in action. We have already seen what happens to these interests when their practical development is inhibited; they merge with the impulse to acquire knowledge and express themselves in thinking, philosophizing. With this in mind, let us supplement our statement of the hypothesis of inhibition by adding: "This barrier causes the practical interests to converge with the impulse to acquire knowledge and thus become impulses to thinking."[1]

We now see that the inhibition hypothesis exactly reverses the causal connexion between unsuitableness for practical life and preponderance of thought which the predominance theory assumes. In the latter the preponderance of thought is regarded as the cause of inaptitude; in the inhibition theory, on the contrary, the preponderance of thought is regarded as a result of the practical inaptitude created by inhibition.

To the essentials of normal practical behaviour which we have already enumerated[2]—viz., the presence of practical interests together with a certain intensity on their part and harmony between them—we must, in order to do justice to the hypothesis of inhibition, add a fourth, namely the absence of factors which impede the normal translation of interest into action, in other words the absence of inhibitive factors.

But in the case of the philosophers—and this is exactly

[1] Cf. p. 20. [2] Cf. p. 97.

what the hypothesis of inhibition postulates—such inhibitive factors do exist; they do prevent interests from finding an outlet in action and thus force them to express themselves in thought, thereby bringing about practical inaptitude with its consequent preponderance of philosophic thought.

It remains for us to examine the hypothesis of inhibition—again from the points of view of *vera causa* and utility in explaining practical inaptitude. We thus ask:—

1. Do such inhibitive factors really exist and, if so, are they to be found in the philosophers?

2. Does the hypothesis of inhibition explain the philosophers' diffidence in, and unsuitableness for, practical life.

If the inhibition hypothesis passes this test we must decide between it and the predominance hypothesis on the basis of the reliability of their respective underlying assumptions and of their respective values in explaining new and hitherto uninvestigated facts in the psychology of philosophers.

CHAPTER XIX

PSYCHICAL INHIBITIONS

An event occurs when all its requirements are fulfilled, *i.e.*, all the factors necessary to its taking place are present. If one of these factors is removed, the event does not take place; if a new one is added, the event may either take place or not, according to the nature of the factor, and in the latter case we speak of the inhibitive effect of the new factor.

Such inhibitive effects often interfere with the events of life. If, for instance, we inoculate a horse with anthrax bacilli it will develop the disease within a short time; if anthrax serum has previously been injected no illness will occur: the serum has inhibited the event for which all the other requirements were fulfilled. A person suffering from diabetes secretes sugar in his urine: if he is given insulin, the secretion is inhibited.

In the nervous system especially, the part played by inhibitions is important, even in the reflexes. A male frog deprived of its cerebrum will croak when stroked gently along its back; it will not croak if at the same time its hind foot is pinched, this irritation having an inhibitive effect on the croaking reflex. A dog with a severed upper spinal cord if stroked lightly on one side of its belly will scratch hard with the corresponding hind leg, but the reflex is inhibited if the dog is touched at another point of its skin at the same time. The knee-tendon reflex will, in many people, only work when their attention is diverted; thus their attention acts as an inhibition of the reflex. A stream of cold water played upon the neck may even act as an inhibition of the breathing reflex.

The instinctive actions are far more exposed to inhibition. Lloyd Morgan says: "A bird that has in early days seized a bee with ill effects is shy for a long time, not only of bees but of moths, large flies and beetles";[1] here the after-effects of an unpleasant experience inhibit the instinct to hunt for insects. A single experience of the evil-tasting cinnabar caterpillar is generally sufficient to prevent chickens from eating them. Cockroaches, which instinctively make for the darkest corners of their habitat, may be permanently deterred from doing so by repeated electric shocks; a dog may be trained not to eat when a particular pitch of the voice is used. In all these cases instinctive actions form the subject of inhibitions which are of a more permanent nature than reflex inhibitions.

Human actions, which after all are also traceable in the long run to instincts, are inhibitable in the same way as those of animals: the burnt child dreads the fire; the instinctive action of touching is inhibited by memory of the pain. The box on the ears which a child receives for an act of disobedience in leaving the pavement for the road has just the same inhibitive effect on the development of future desires of the same kind as

[1] p. 54.

the electric shock had on the cockroaches. All punishments inflicted in the process of education have this inhibitive effect on intended actions; all unlearning of things once learned is based on the inhibitive effect of unpleasant experiences, and much of what is learned through experience, especially the abstention from purposeless actions, is also the work of inhibition.

The psychical life of the normal human being is thus beset at all points by inhibitive processes and, though we have said above that the fourth requirement for normal behaviour in practical life is the absence of inhibitive factors, we cannot regard this as literally true. Normal practical behaviour is, on the contrary, impossible without inhibitive factors. But this apparent contradiction will soon be solved.

The objects of inhibition are the impulses to act; what then are its instruments? What are the inhibitive factors? It has often been contended that the impulses are found in couples of opposites—pugnacity, for example, being paired with fear, exhibitionist desires with shame, and hunger with nausea; thus impulses to action would be found on one side and tendencies of an inhibitive kind on the other. Although it is not possible to give this theory general application, the assumption which it makes as to the presence of inhibitive instincts is a correct one.

Animals experience a purely instinctive form of fear, *i.e.*, one which is unconnected with unpleasant experiences—for example, the fear of the antelope for the tiger, that of the three or four-day-old chicken for larger animals or human beings, or the fear exhibited by Köhler's chimpanzees on seeing a picture of a Cingalese demon. This fear also seems to occur in children and young people when brought into early or sudden contact with sexual life. Fear, being connected with the desire to escape, is strictly an impulse towards action, but it often operates not as such but merely as an inhibition of other impulses towards action, as when it prevents a chicken from eating a large beetle or holds young people back from following their sexual inclinations.

A further inhibitive instinct is shame, which, though originating in the sexual sphere, penetrates far into the other spheres of life. It is often a check upon sexual tendencies but it also has an inhibitive effect on the reflexes of the bladder and intestines; it sets a limit to the development of purely selfish interests in professional, social and public life and often acts as a curb upon ambition by holding people back from public activities.

Nausea, originally serving the purpose of preventing unsuitable or too rich food from being eaten, also operates to restrain from contact with excrement and dirt and thus forms a most valuable factor of cleanliness; in the sphere of sex it operates as an inhibitive factor, and it plays a part as such in social matters, especially between people of different classes or races. When sublimated and complicated by association with the pugnacious instincts, it introduces, in the form of contempt, still further inhibitive factors into human relations.

Finally, we may class among the inhibitive instincts that of fatigue. Its effects, though very general, are however only temporary.

As we have so far spoken only of instincts, we have

still left unmentioned the strongest inhibitive factor in psychical life, pain. Pain operates in the first place as an inhibition of all actions which bring it about: William James says very truly: " . . . it is almost impossible for a man to cut or mutilate himself slowly and deliberately —his hand invincibly refusing to bring on the pain."[1] But the effect of pain goes beyond the mere inhibition of the action itself; future actions of the same or a similar kind are inhibited, even in intention, after one or more painful experiences; consequently we may say that pain has a permanently inhibitive effect, as we have already shewn in the examples given above. This effect may come into operation without any recollection of the previous unpleasant experiences. When adding up a sum we do not bear in mind the circumstances in which we learned to add, and it is just as unnecessary that, for instance, a child which has once been induced through punishment to give up the habit of biting its nails when writing or of picking its nose when reading should remember the punishments inflicted for these offences in order to continue to refrain from them; the memory will act subconsciously. On the other hand, memories of this kind—*e.g.*, of a burn or the bite of a dog—*may* assert themselves, and then their inhibitive effect will often be greatly intensified by the additional operation of fear. This fear, which, contrary to that mentioned above, is derived from painful experiences, is sometimes completely disproportionate to the pain which has really been suffered and is expected again, as for example when a patient who has once had a hypodermic injection is so

[1] Vol. II, p. 550.

afraid of the stab of the needle that he cannot face a second one.

Thus, not only pain and the fear of pain but also all kinds of physically unpleasant sensations, such as heat or cold, nausea, or shortness of breath, constitute permanent inhibitions of the actions by means of which they are brought about. Nor is the situation different in the case of unpleasant sensations arising from psychical causes—the sensations of boredom, loneliness, loss of dignity, and the feelings associated with failure in profession, love, society, or politics. All these, and the fear of them, have an inhibitive effect upon our actions and can, if they arise from deeply felt or repeated experiences, even go so far as to crush the spirit of enterprise completely.

The inhibitive factors of our psychical life are thus in part instincts, such as fear, shame and nausea, in part feelings of dislike, such as pain, anxiety and boredom, and in part vestigiary memories of unpleasant experiences. Since, however, the effect, even in the case of inhibitive instincts, is produced by unpleasant sensations, we may say in a general way that sensations of displeasure are the inhibitive factors of the mind; this, however, must not be erroneously regarded as meaning that unpleasant sensations can have inhibitive effects only and no stimulating ones.

From all these considerations we may draw the conclusion that psychical inhibitions do undoubtedly exist and are of decisive importance for our actions—indeed for the whole development of our capacities and our character. And that is all I propose to demonstrate here, for it by no means lies in my intention to give a full account of inhibitive factors and their effects.

After the reality and the importance of the psychical inhibitions, another of their characteristics—that of intensity—is of chief interest to us. The above-mentioned pathological illustrations of immunity from anthrax and the effect of insulin, show how important is the *quantity* of the inhibitive factor: too little serum will not prevent the outbreak of the disease; too little insulin will only reduce the secretion of sugar without stopping it. Consequently the process of inhibition is, in this latter case, capable of regulation at will. The intensity of an inhibition is therefore measured by the material quantity or energic volume of the phenomena which it inhibits; the less this is, the greater the inhibition. Such exact experiments or observations as have been made in the physiological field have not yet been made in that of psychology but there are good reasons to believe that the psychical inhibitive factors also operate with varying degrees of intensity.

Different individuals are affected to quite different extents; some are more inhibited, others less. But how are we to measure or even estimate the degree of inhibition? Since we are concerned with the inhibition of action, of activity, what could be simpler than to base our conclusions on the amount of activity observed and say: the more active a person is, the less he is inhibited, the less active, the more inhibited? But we already know from the discussion of the passivity of the philosophers that this conclusion is not a safe one. Passivity may just as well be due to the absence, weakness or disharmony of the interests as to particularly intense inhibitions. We must therefore seek other criteria for the intensity of inhibitions.

1. Inhibitive factors need not be subjectively noticeable, as we have already seen; they can do their work without awakening memories of unpleasant experiences or creating consciousness of their inhibitive influence *per se* through a specific sensation or experience of inhibition. But this subjective effect *may* come about; such inhibitions, such feelings or rather sensations of being inhibited, do exist, and their intensity furnishes the first point on which to base an estimate of the intensity of the inhibitions themselves.

Some people experience unusually intense inhibitions of this kind. Thus Ranke writes in his *Biography:* "You will understand and agree that in the end I refused this offer (a call to Göttingen) as well. There were reasons for and against, but what decided me was a quite categorical inner voice which said 'no.'"[1] C. F. Meyer, the well-known Swiss poet, said of himself: "I was *bound by a powerful spell;* I no longer lived. I was *fixed in a dream.*"[2] And Grillparzer wrote: "It is true that I passed my time from 18 to 25 in a similar state of *stupefaction* and inactivity."[3] Such feelings lead us to assume that strong inhibitions were at work, and the inactivity which is expressed in the two last quotations furnishes confirmation of this assumption.

[1] *Zur eigenen Lebensgeschichte*, pp. 302 ff; quoted from O. Apelt's translation of *Theaetetus*, note 13, *Plato*, IV

[2] Birnbaum, p. 135 (my italics).

[3] *Ibid.*, p. 142 (my italics).

2. We shall assume inhibitions to be more intense in proportion to their *permanence*. The inhibition, for example, which arises out of the chicken's unfortunate experience with the cinnabar caterpillar and lasts for its whole life must owe this persistence to its extreme intensity. In the same way, when a person is prevented by disappointment, anger, or disgust from ever repeating the experiment which caused him these unpleasant feelings in spite of his interest in the matter, we shall find it simplest to ascribe the persistence of the inhibition to an exceptionally intense inhibitive experience.

3. We have recognized as an inhibitive factor of especial importance the fear arising from unpleasant experiences. If a person is exceptionally timid, avoids even remote possibilities of harm, or definitely suffers from morbid accesses of fear, we must expect to find especially strong inhibitions. But such people will also furnish evidence that their activity is severely impaired. The confession of the seventeenth-century mystic, Hans Engelbrecht, may serve as an example. He says: "I learnt the trade of varnish-making for three years, but I *could not do much good at it* on account of my great *anxiety of soul* and sadness."[1] Again, the famous physician and author, I. G. Zimmermann, wrote in a letter: "It (melancholy) is due to the *great anxiety which accompanies it* . . . and *the infinite effort which I have to make* if I have to write a letter, read a page, or pay a visit after the first hour of the day."[2]

[1] Birnbaum, p. 147 (my italics).
[2] *Ibid.*, p. 137 (my italics).

4. Shame, as we have seen, is an inhibitive factor which, though it does not play so important a part as fear, has nevertheless extensive and powerful effects. Thus a person in whom this instinct is highly developed will, like the person suffering from fear, have especially strong inhibitions. An intense and highly developed sense of shame is called shyness and we may therefore expect to find shy people subject to intense inhibitions. This expectation is fully supported by the well-known passivity of such people, their diffidence in their profession, in their love-affairs, and in society, and their abstention from public life.

5. A fifth symptom of unusually strong inhibitions is displayed in the tendency to hesitate, in constitutional indecision. It arises, just as awkwardness does, when a person overstresses negative considerations—and these are, after all, the inhibitive ones, with which we deal in all important decisions in life and in many minor decisions as well—at the expense of positive considerations, which can make themselves felt only after a long and arduous struggle, if at all, however insistent or convincing they may be. Such a person will be prone to call to his aid fixed principles devised to rid him once and for all of the pains of doubt, or he will resort to such out-of-the-way expedients as divination, and dream-reading, or, if he is of a scientific turn of mind, to Franklin's arithmetic —that is, he will allot marks to the reasons for and against the action and strike the balance.

6. Lastly, we know that easy and undisturbed working of the psychical functions is pleasurable, whereas difficult

and impeded working is unpleasurable. Hence to the extent to which a given individual's inhibitions are stronger than normal, his whole temperament and outlook will tend to sadness, depression and melancholy.

Therefore, the presence of a disposition of this kind is further evidence of particularly intense inhibitions. The frequency with which a depressed temperament and impaired activity occur together—particularly noticeable in pathological cases—furnishes a valuable confirmation of the correctness of tracing depressed temperaments back to intense inhibitions.

Intense awareness of inhibition, its persistence, fear, shyness, indecision and a depressed temperament are thus the symptoms from which we conclude that the person exhibiting them suffers from exceptional intensity of inhibition, the more certainly when several of the symptoms occur together or when they are found associated with impaired activity. The opposite type, the person with few inhibitions, will on the contrary, be characterized by the absence of awareness of inhibition, adventurousness, impudence, decision, a cheerful temperament and great activity. Wm. James says very aptly in this connexion: "He (the man free from inhibitions) will be the king of his company, sing all the songs, make all the speeches, lead the parties, carry out the practical jokes, kiss all the girls, fight the men, and, if need be, lead the forlorn hopes and enterprises, so that an onlooker would think he has more life in his little finger than can exist in the whole body of a correct judicious fellow. But the judicious fellow all the while may have all these possibilities and more besides, ready to break out in the same or even a more violent way if only the brakes were taken off." [1]

Exceptionally strong inhibitions lead to a greater or lesser restriction of action which may go as far as complete inactivity; exceptionally slight inhibitions lead to a surplus of activity and a state of great busyness, which may go as far as frenzied excitement. A certain intermediate strength of inhibitions is thus one of the requisites of normal practical behaviour. This is the solution of the apparent paradox which we have already considered, whereby on the one hand the absence of inhibitive factors and on the other hand their presence was necessary to normal behaviour. In point of fact, the absence of intense inhibitions which restrain the action-impulses is essential, but equally essential is the presence of normal ones which keep them within bounds.

What is the reason for the difference of intensity in the inhibitions of different people? We found the seat of inhibitive forces in unpleasurable emotions; it might be possible that unpleasurable emotions of the same strength should for some unknown reason give rise in different people to inhibitions of very different intensity; it might also be possible for the average intensity of the unpleasurable emotions themselves to differ with different individuals so that the person with slight inhibitions would be one with but slightly developed unpleasurable emotions—in other words, insensitive, thick-skinned—whilst the person with strong inhibitions would owe his temperament to a tendency to strong emotions of displeasure and be highly strung, easily upset and hyper-

[1] Vol. II, p. 538.

sensitive. We shall see later that such variations of sensitiveness do in point of fact occur as causes of individual differences in the intensity of inhibition, but we will not on that account reject the possibility that in other cases the first-named phenomenon may also occur.

The inhibitive factors, however, are capable not only of varying in intensity as between different individuals, so that it is possible to distinguish "inhibited" and "uninhibited" types, but they may also immensely change their intensity in the same individual. An otherwise timid person may suddenly perform a foolhardy act, a shy person not infrequently has a sudden access of brazenness, an awkward one may occasionally display great adroitness, an undecided one take a decision on the spur of the moment, or a depressed person become hilarious. This change may be quite transient or it may last for some time; long accesses of increased inhibition may follow those of slight inhibition and vice versa, and these periods may even occur at regular periods.

The causes of this change of temperament vary. Firstly, age plays a part. A child is far less subject to inhibitions than an adult; a young person—apart from the period of puberty—than an old one. Secondly, health: even slight physical or psychical disturbances may greatly increase inhibitions. Thirdly, external circumstances, especially success and failure, respectively decrease and increase them; success goes to the head, intoxicates, that is to say, it reduces inhibitions; failure depresses. Fourthly and lastly, there are other and unknown inner factors which have a quite decisive effect upon the intensity of inhibition; it is these which, independently of all other factors, bring about the depressing and enlivening phases of life; in the extremes of melancholy and mania, with the immensely increased inhibitions which characterize the former and the complete absence of inhibition in the latter state, we see these inner factors at work, pathologically magnified.

The results of the considerations set forth in this long chapter may be summed up as follows:—

1. Psychical factors exist which inhibit the impulses to action;

2. Inhibitive factors are of great importance in normal psychical life;

3. The effects of inhibition vary in different people;

4. The inhibitions reach different intensity in the same person at different times.

CHAPTER XX

PHILOSOPHERS AS PEOPLE WITH INTENSE INHIBITIONS

We wished to test the inhibition hypothesis which says that the unsuitableness of philosophers for the practical affairs of life arises from an inhibition of practical interests. We have seen that such psychical inhibitions exist, but we have also seen that they are essentially factors of normal psychical existence and are thus found in all normal people. Nevertheless, normal people are not unfitted for practical affairs and we cannot therefore ascribe such unfitness to inhibitions pure and simple. We must ascribe it, if at all, to unusually strong inhibitions. In this more precise form the inhibition hypothesis would consequently be expressed thus: the unsuitableness of the philosophers for practical life arises from unusually intense inhibitions which greatly reduce the possible outlets of the practical impulses in action and thus force them into an alternative activity, that of philosophic thought. In order to establish this hypothesis it will be necessary to prove, not that the philosophers were subject to inhibitions of impulses to action—for that is obviously the case, though it explains nothing—but that they suffered from exceptionally active, especially intense and abnormally strong inhibitions. Can this proof be found?

Socrates speaks in several passages[1] of the Platonic dialogues of a divine sign which prevents him from carrying out the action which he intended to perform. It is like a voice at his side, forbidding him to do what he intended to do. In the *Phaedrus* he relates that this sign—which he calls his "daemon"—held him back from crossing a bridge and thus beginning his homeward journey, in the *Euthydemos* it similarly prevented him from leaving the dressing-room of the Lyceum, in the *Apology* he says that it often stopped him in the middle of a speech, in the *Theaetetus* that it forbade him to have social relations with any of his pupils, in *Alcibiades I* that it prevented him for years from addressing Alcibiades, and in the *Republic* and more explicitly in the *Apology*, he explains that it always held him back from political life. Thus, whether momentarily or permanently, both in important and in unimportant matters, it made itself felt—but always impeding, never assisting. "It always forbids me to do something which I am going to do,"[2] he says in the *Phaedrus*. And in the *Apology* he writes: "This sign I have had ever since I was a child. The sign is a voice which comes to me and always forbids me to do something which I am going to do, but never commands me to do anything, and this is what stands in the way of my being a politician."[3]

What is this mysterious daemon? A warning voice, says Socrates himself—but not the voice of reason, for when it prevented him, for example, as we are told in

[1] *Apology*, 31 D, 40 B; *Phaedrus*, 242; *Euthydemos*, 272 E; *Republic*, 496; *Theaetetus*, 151 A.; *Euthyphron*, 3 B; *Alcibiades*, I, 103, 124 c.

[2] 242.

[3] 31 D.

the *Euthydemos*, from leaving the Lyceum, there was no question of sensible reflexion but only of a—perhaps quite unconscious—wish or expectation that some further interesting experience awaited him. Nor was it the voice of conscience, for the actions which it prevented were in no way unethical. Nor was it, again, "a practical tact, a keen feeling for what was suitable to his own individuality"[1] as Apelt suggests, for such a feeling must necessarily also have expressed itself positively, in counsel: this, however, is exactly what it never did; it always warned and checked—"it always forbids me to do something which I am going to do." What is this but an intensive inhibition—a reawakening of earlier unpleasant experiences which, though no longer remembered as such, condense their whole repressive power into a sensation of inhibition which only differs in its extreme intensity from similar sensations felt by normal beings? The statement of Socrates that he heard a voice at his side need not necessarily be regarded as a simile, for intense experiences of this kind, whether dissuasive or persuasive, may at times, even in mentally healthy people, take the form of inner voices, as Ranke reports of himself in the quotation given above. I myself—and I hope I am not mentally ailing—have heard, at least once in my life when in a situation of perplexity, an inner voice which loudly said "yes." Socrates, therefore, was a man with intense sensations of inhibition, the effectiveness of which corresponded completely to their subjective intensity, for he obeyed them unquestioningly in all vital issues—in word and in deed. The melancholy

[1] Translation of *Theaetetus*, note 13.

temperament with which tradition credits him may be adduced as further evidence of this fact.

Plato, according to the report of Aristotle, was also a melancholy man; in addition, he was extremely cautious, even timid. He took the greatest care to ensure that none of his views on God should penetrate to the masses. He therefore adhered externally with the greatest strictness to the traditional religion; he supported, in his *Laws*, the old respect for the gods and, in his second letter to Dionysius, ventured only upon "riddles" as to the problem of the nature of divinity, ". . . so that, if anything happens to the letter on land or sea, anyone who reads it may not understand."[1] And even the riddles seemed to him dangerous, for he warns the recipient to "burn this letter when you have read it through several times."[2] This caution was also the main reason for his remaining aloof from the affairs of the Athenian State in spite of his impassioned interest in politics. Referring unmistakably to himself, he says in the *Republic*: ". . . he (the politician) will be like a man that has fallen among wild beasts—unwilling to join in their iniquities and unable to resist the fury of all, and therefore destined to perish . . .;—having, I say, weighed all this, such a man keeps quiet and confines himself to his own concerns like one who takes shelter behind a wall on a stormy day, when the wind is driving before it a hurricane of dust and rain. . . ."[3] A further proof of the intensity of his inhibitions is furnished by the fact that, as a youth, he burnt his tragedies instead of publishing them. Plato also, we may assume

[1] *Ep.* II, 312 D. [2] *Ep.* II, 314 C. [3] 496.

from all this, was a man with extremely intense inhibitions.

Of Aristotle we have too little certain knowledge to draw conclusions regarding such intimate processes as inhibitions. It is, nevertheless, probable that his famous phrase that all men of genius are melancholy men was not evolved without reference to his own case and, in consequence, that he had a temperament of this kind. On the other hand, his flight from Athens cannot be regarded as a sign of undue timidity; it was a measure dictated purely by the instinct of self-preservation, for the charge of impiety must necessarily have led to the infliction of the death penalty upon a man of his political views.

St Augustine tells us how, in his early thirties, he was only able to continue his accustomed existence at the price of ever-increasing anxiety, until at last the painful conflict was solved after a tremendous emotional storm by the decision to withdraw completely from love and the world. The entire suppression of these interests speaks for the immense intensity of the inhibition associated with his anxiety.

Bruno was subject to fits of depression which were capable of attaining the stage of a longing for death. "*In tristitia hilaris, in hilaritate tristis*," is his description of himself. "Even early in life," says Riehl, "he longed for the end of a life-work full of storms, for bed, quiet repose and the 'certain rest' of death."[1]

Descartes, at the age of 23, underwent, like St Augustine, an intense inner crisis characterized by a high degree of

[1] p. 55.

hypochondria and anxiety. Uncertainty and doubts beset him, deep depression preyed upon his mind, and he was shaken by fearsome dreams. He, too, thought first of turning from the practical to the mystic life ; he attempted to establish relations with the Rosicrucians, but was unsuccessful. It was another avenue of escape from the turmoil of life—namely, passionate devotion to science—that led him to freedom. He was just as anxious as Plato not to give rise to any kind of scandal in religious matters. He decided first of all to keep his ideas to himself and not even to write them down, then he decided to put them in writing for his own use, and it was only very gradually and under the influence of other scholars that he approached the plan of publication, which he immediately relinquished when he heard of the condemnation of Galileo. It took three years—until after he had turned 40—before he at last ventured to publish his first work, but the work in question, far from being the already planned and partly written cosmology, with its heretical teachings concerning the formation of the heavenly bodies and the movement of the earth, was the harmless *Discourse*, together with *Geometry*, *Dioptrics* and *Meteors*. Not until eight years later did he publish the *Principles of Philosophy*, in which these dangerous teachings were, it is true, contained; but that of the formation of the heavenly bodies was put forward as not being meant seriously, whilst that of the movement of the earth was weakened and expressed in guarded phrases.

Locke was 54 before he overcame his undue cautiousness and shyness to the extent of publishing anything, though he had long since committed to paper, at all events in outline, many of his thoughts and also the *Essay concerning Human Understanding*. One of the first of these publications, the *Letter concerning Toleration*, he kept carefully anonymous and he nearly broke off his friendship with Limborch for dropping some hints on the matter. This caution is the subject of comment by Thomas Burnett of Kemnay, who wrote in a letter to Leibniz: "Mr Locke is known here as a man who, more than another, meditates and reflects upon what he writes, especially in philosophy. He weighs and weighs again, he looks at everything from the front, the back, and the side, so that he must always have an advantage over anyone who does not consider everything so exactly. . . ."[1] He was just as cautious in practical life, in giving introductions and advice; we know that such unusual caution suggests very intense inhibitions.

Spinoza, again, behaved in similar fashion; the only work which he published himself in his whole life, the *Tractatus Theologico-politicus* appeared without the author's name and gave a false place of printing. Shortly before his death, Colerus reports, he burned a Dutch translation of the Pentateuch. He even left instructions that his legacies should be distributed anonymously. His placidity and self-control also point to intense inhibition. "His passions," said Colerus, "were wonderfully under control. No one ever saw him too sad or too merry."[2]

Leibniz says the same thing of himself: "He will

[1] Fechtner, p. 286. [2] Gebhard, p. 69.

never be seen unusually merry or unusually sad."[1] He also says that he is cautious or timid: "He is afraid to undertake an affair but bold to execute it."[1] This is a particularly characteristic remark and shows that the inhibitions of action were intense but when they were once overcome the pent-up energy asserted itself strongly. The picture of a greatly-inhibited man is completed by timidity in social matters: "I am the victim of a deficiency which is counted for much in the world at large, namely that of social manners, and I thereby spoil the first impression which I make,"[2] he wrote to Lichtenstein.

Hume, again, frequently emphasizes his shyness; as a young man he found that it made him unsuitable to be a travelling tutor, and thirteen years later he speaks of himself in his *Character of ——, written by himself*, as still "very bashful" and "a gallant who gives no offence to husbands and mothers."[3] As a writer he was, like Plato and Descartes, greatly afraid of giving scandal in matters of religion. His *Treatise of Human Nature* originally contained a chapter on miracles which he sent one day to the philosopher Henry Home, with a warning not to show it to anyone and to burn it when read: "I am at present castrating my work, that is, cutting off its nobler parts; that is, endeavouring it shall give as little offence as possible, before which, I could not pretend to put it into the Doctor's hands. This is a piece of cowardice, for which I blame myself. . . ."[4] The chapter

[1] Fischer, III, p. 294.
[2] *Ibid.*, p. 111.
[3] Burton, Vol. I, p. 226.
[4] *Ibid.*, Vol. I, p. 64.

in question also fell a victim to "castration." He became somewhat more courageous later when he ventured to publish works on religious philosophy, but he always kept a back door open and at times attacked his own views and even the harmless doctrine of deism in order to shew his reverence for the State Church and theism. He remained true, moreover, to the practice of "castration"; for he caused to be removed and destroyed the two essays, *Suicide* and *The Immortality of the Soul*, which had been set up ready for printing as part of his last philosophic publication, *The Natural History of Religion*. And finally, he could not summon up courage to continue his *Dialogues concerning Natural Religion* although he himself found that "nothing can be more cautiously or more artfully written," and although he was well aware that little harm could come to him, for he had but a few more months to live. He thought, nevertheless, that he was too open in what he wrote, in spite of being "cautious in his words, still more so in his actions." At 18, he fell a victim to a nervous ailment which for the next few years was associated with severe depression and which the consolations of philosophy were unable to assuage.

Rousseau, though one of the most passionate and excitable, was also one of the most inhibited of the great thinkers; that these qualities are not mutually exclusive he himself proves by the numerous detailed and highly illuminating accounts of his inhibitions, which are found in his *Confessions*. His shyness was so intense as to prevent him from performing the simplest and most everyday tasks if he felt himself under observation.

"A thousand times, whilst I was an apprentice and afterwards, I have gone out with the intention of buying some sweetmeat or other. I approach the confectioner's shop; I see women at the counter; I believe that they are laughing and joking with one another at the little sugar-baby. I pass a fruit-stall and cast glances at the nice pears, their fragrance attracts me; two or three young people standing near look at me; a man who knows me is standing at the door of his shop; . . . my short-sightedness causes me a thousand illusions. Every passer-by seems to be an acquaintance and I am always rendered diffident, *restrained by some obstacle;* my longing grows with my hesitancy and finally I go home like a fool, consumed with desire."[1] Because he had delayed a visit for a few days, fear of fulfilling his duty so late made him afraid to pay it at all. This diffidence was particularly noticeable where women were concerned; it was extraordinarily difficult for him to make the acquaintance of women and in their company he was often so awkward and stupid that they soon lost interest in him. When in love these characteristics were increased to the point of distraction and in situations of a certain delicacy he was frequently unable to take the lead. Never, even in the most impassioned love-encounters, did he dare to admit his masochistic perversion to a woman. When once an Italian girl, whom he ardently desired and whose room he had entered, told him to sit at her feet, he threw himself down, trembling, with a cry: "But what will hardly be believed is that I dared attempt no more, not even to say a single word, to raise my eyes to

[1] Bk. I (p. 47—my italics).

her, even in my awkward position to touch her by leaning an instant against her knee. I was dumb and motionless, but certainly not calm; everything in me betrayed my agitation. . . ."[1] At the time of this scene Rousseau was 16 years old, but he behaved in exactly the same way some thirty years later towards the woman whom he loved most passionately, Mme d'Houdetot. "We had supped together and we were alone in a grove in the moonlight and after two hours of the most vivacious and tender conversation she went at midnight out of the grove and her friend's arms as untouched, as pure in body and heart as she had gone in. Reader, ponder all the circumstances! I will add nothing to them. And do not think that my senses left me as much alone as if I had been with Thérèse or my mother. I have already said it: this was love, love in all its strength and all its fury."[2] In Rousseau, diffidence combined with fear to create an inhibition which stood in his way in all his relations with other people. "Everything makes me shy and afraid; a passing fly frightens me; a word that I ought to speak, a movement that I ought to make, has first to overcome my inertia. *Fear and shame* rule me to such a degree that I should like to hide from every one's sight. If there is something to be done, I do not know how to begin it, if there is something to be said I am at a loss to know what to say, if anyone looks at me, I am put out of countenance."[3] These conditions made it impossible for him to speak freely and for fear of this he did not dare to appear before the consistory to answer

[1] Bk. II (p. 84).
[2] Bk. IX (p. 220).
[3] Bk. I (p. 46—my italics).

the charge of disbelief; nor could he face an audience with the King, the result of which would probably have been the grant of a pension. He was very cautious in love-affairs, which he allowed to become the occasion of so much worry and mystery-making that most of them failed on that very account. In other ways, too, he was prone to anxiety; we have already seen that he regarded every situation as fraught with the worst possible consequences and in his youth the fear of Hell caused him for some time the most cruel torments. He was continuously subject to slight or severe hypochondria, which began at the age of 24: he describes the state of passivity which accompanied it in the following characteristic words: "I was growing accustomed to languishing, to going without sleep, to thinking instead of acting, ..."[1] Thinking instead of acting—this is, in truth, the inevitable result of inhibitions of so far-reaching a kind.

Kant, with his punctiliousness, his precisely ordered life and his habit of acting in accordance with fixed principles—in diametrical opposition to the disorderly, adventurous, and impulsive Rousseau—resembled him, nevertheless, in the point which interests us here—the intensity of inhibition. He did not fail to elevate his caution as a writer into a general principle. In connexion with his dispute with the Prussian Government, he wrote on a piece of paper found among his effects: "Though everything which one writes must be true, it is not on that account a duty to publish every truth."[2] He followed this principle, to which he often gave utterance,

[1] Bk. VI (p. 14).

[2] Paulsen, *Kant*, p. 50.

when, faced by the royal threat of "disagreeable measures" in case of further misuse of his philosophy for attacks upon Christianity, he drew back alarmed and declared with all solemnity that he would in future "refrain absolutely from all public lectures and writings regarding religion, whether natural or revealed."[1] Paulsen remarks aptly in this connexion: "After all, at 70, he might have let the threatened 'disagreeable measures' take their course; Berlin would hardly have done more than forbid the works concerned and possibly also cancel his supplementary allowances."[2] In view of his considerable fortune, he could have afforded to submit to the latter punishment without complaint. But we also find in other aspects of his life signs of exaggerated anxiety: he was particularly afraid of causing damage of any kind. When, for example, his servant once broke a wineglass, he asked that the splinters should be buried so that nobody might be cut by them. He did not, however, venture to entrust the task to his servant but asked his guests to perform it. So they went out into the garden and looked for a sufficiently unfrequented spot. Kant, however, objected to every proposal "on the ground that someone might hurt himself, until at length a spot was found by the side of an old wall and a deep hole dug in which the splinters were carefully buried in our presence."[3] He also seems to have been something of a waverer; twice, as we have seen, he intended to make a proposal of marriage and on both occasions he allowed the opportunity to pass as the result of indecision. He himself describes

[1] Kant, *Streit der Fakultäten* (*Werke*, V, p. 52). [2] p. 51.
[3] Jachmann, p. 142.

his melancholy temperament graphically in a letter to Hufeland: "I have, owing to my flat and contracted breast which gives scant room to the beating of the heart and the action of the lungs, a natural tendency to hypochondria, which in my earlier life bordered on a disgust for life itself."[1] And the inhibitions which accompany this "hypochondria" are also clear in his mind, for he continues: "And as a man rejoices more in life from what he does freely of his own accord than from what he enjoys, so can intellectual effort oppose another kind of the *feeling* or sensation of life to the restrictions which are purely physical."[2] Inhibitions due to unpleasant experiences were enormously persistent in his mind. Jachmann relates that Kant once went for a drive with a Count. This lasted longer than he liked, with the result that he only arrived home at 10 o'clock. He at once evolved the rule never to travel in a carriage unless he had hired it himself and could consequently do what he liked with it. "As soon as this rule had been made, he knew exactly what he would do in a similar case and nothing in the world would have made him abandon his principle."[2] For many years he was in the habit of supping every Saturday with others at his friend Green's house; when Green died Kant never again supped in company and even gave up the habit of taking an evening meal.

Hegel, even externally, gave those about him the impression of being a man with strong inhibitions. At 19, there was already something old and slow in his character so that his fellow-students called him "the

[1] Birnbaum, p. 264. [2] *Idem*, p. 149.

old man." One of them even drew a caricature of him, showing him walking painfully on crutches, with the inscription: "May God be kind to an old man." It is also significant that he wrote two essays on current politics, at the age of 26 and 29, but never printed them; what inhibitions gave rise to these decisions we do not know, but that they were potent ones is clear from their effect, since it is usually difficult for anyone, and for a philosopher most of all, to decide against printing what is already written.

The inability to make up his mind to finish and publish his work was particularly noticeable in Schelling's later years, and assumed quite unique forms in view of the clash between the promises and announcements which he made at repeated intervals throughout decades and the complete absence of performance. In 1811, Schelling when 36 years old was to have published a large work, the fruit of many years of thought, entitled *The Ages of the World*. It was to have been ready at Easter and the first book was already printed; Schelling, however, stopped its publication. At Whitsuntide he proposed to spend the whole summer on it but in spite of the greatest interest in his theme—"it is a pet child for which I am caring," he wrote—it did not advance; in winter he complained that the subject was too wide and the work too much; moreover, hypochondriacal moods were hampering him, but it would "quite certainly" appear for Easter, 1812. Instead, he announced at the end of the year that it would be published in the following one. War broke out in that year and Schelling consoled himself with the thought that the times were not propitious for his work; after the war, however, it would not be long in appearing. The catalogue of the Leipzig Fair for 1815 reported the *Ages of the World* as published, but in point of fact Schelling had withdrawn the work for a second time, after fifteen sheets had already been set up in type. Four years later he admitted that he was still unable to bring himself to put the finishing touches to the work, because it was not, to his mind, a complete success. In 1821 he announced his intention to print his lectures on mythology, but failed to do so; in 1822 he wrote to a friend that he hoped to send them to him, printed, in the following year. Four years later he made the same promise to Victor Cousin; the book was once more included in the Fair catalogue and once more Schelling withdrew a considerable part of it after it had been set up. Ten years later it was again announced, but, although the matter had by then become a public scandal, Schelling never allowed the book to appear, any more than the *Ages of the World*, of which in any case only the first book had ever existed. In fact, after the age of 40, Schelling published practically nothing. He attributed this insurmountable diffidence, this "undue anxiety," in the matter of publication to dissatisfaction with the products of his mind; they did not reach the standard which he laid down for himself: the inhibitive effect of this dissatisfaction in any case was far above normal intensity. Schelling's own conjecture was that this anxiety arose out of the states of depression which he repeatedly experienced; the first was connected with the death of Caroline Schlegel's daughter, whom he dearly loved, and it clouded his mind—weighed down already with worry and self-reproach—to the point of causing him to contemplate suicide. He was then 25 years old. Ten years later he again complained of fits of hypochondria which prevented him from working and these subsequently became worse, lasted for over ten years and then gradually grew less frequent. In 1821 he wrote to Creuzer: "It is perhaps a vestige of the hypochondria from which I suffered for so many years, in consequence of unpleasant and ugly external circumstances, that makes me unduly anxious, for, although conquered to a fair extent, it is still not completely so."[1]

We hear of Herbart, also, that during his stay at Jena from the age of 18 to 21 he went through a period of deep depression accompanied by ideas of suicide.

If Schelling's inhibitions were connected mainly with his writings, those of Schopenhauer chiefly affected his everyday life—as we might expect, having regard to his far more noticeable unsuitability for it. Any decision, weighty or trifling, was terribly difficult and in a letter to her nineteen-year-old son his mother reproaches him for his "noble indecision which everybody knows." It was also expressed in his year-long reflexions on the various plans which he formed for marriage, and a particularly drastic example is furnished by a schematic comparison of the respective advantages of Frankfurt and Mannheim found on the cover of his book of accounts for 1833. It was evidently intended to facilitate a

[1] Fischer, VII, p. 166.

choice between the two towns. I reproduce this very characteristic list of pros and cons[1] :—

Frankfurt	*Mannheim*
Healthy climate	Good climate (unbearable heat)
Beautiful surroundings	Quiet and no crowds (crowd at the theatre and at meals)
Pleasures of a large town	More respected
Variety of a large town	Better foreign bookshops
Better reading room	The music society and library
Natural history museum	Heidelberg library
Better theatre, opera, and concerts	A really social club
More Englishmen	Better bathing in summer
Better cafés	Big saving on books
Senckenberg library	Less chance of being robbed
No floods	Able to keep a maid later on
Less observed	No great rush anywhere (theatre)
Friendly town and neighbourhood	Able to keep a better table later on
Less tied down, less bothered with social engagements due to accident rather than choice, possibility of avoiding and cutting undesired social ties	A very good place for supper
Clever dentist and few bad doctors	
Not so unbearably hot in summer	
The *physikalisches Kabinett*	

Unpleasant experiences, even though they had only happened once, created inhibitions of extraordinary persistence. If his impression of a person at their first meeting was unfavourable or even associated with some

[1] v. Gwinner, p. 242.

unpleasant happening, he was afraid of ever crossing that person's path again: this happened with Schleiermacher and with Byron. Anxiety, exaggerated caution and unhealthy mistrust were developed in Schopenhauer's character to an extraordinary degree. He was, indeed, afraid of everybody and everything, of imaginary dangers just as much as of real ones. As a youth he persuaded himself that he suffered from all kinds of ailments or that he might become involved in disputes. When war broke out he feared that he might be forced to serve. He fled from smallpox at Naples and from cholera at Berlin. He always had daggers and loaded pistols at his bedside. He concealed his valuables in the most unlikely places, he made his business notes in English, or if they were particularly important, in Latin or Greek. He was perpetually afraid of being exploited, cheated or robbed. His sister urged upon him to make an arrangement with their common debtor who was in financial difficulties; Schopenhauer at once angrily maintained that the man had been given unduly favourable terms, and his mistrust and her mortification led to his ceasing relations with his sister for ten years. The great friend of his youth, Grégoire de Blésimare, with whom he had resumed relations of friendship after an interruption lasting for twenty years, advised him not to put his money into a life-insurance company but to invest it through Blésimare himself; Schopenhauer at once suspected selfish motives and broke off the relations which had just been resumed. He was often subject, sometimes without reason, to morbid fears. As a six-year-old child his parents returned from a walk to find him in a state of utter despair, believing that they had left him for ever. As a youth he was subject to nocturnal fears; when in 1833 he proposed to leave Mannheim, he was again tormented by fear. Not until the coming of old age did these attacks grow less. They were closely associated with the tendency to depression from which, like so many other thinkers, Schopenhauer suffered. At 17, the hated pursuit of business brought deep depression with it; this was increased by his father's death to a condition of unrelieved gloom which lasted for two years and "was but little removed from real melancholia."[1] Seven years later he was again "suffering deeply in mind and cast down,"[2] because he believed that he was living at an epoch which called for quite different gifts from his own. At 43, shortly after removing to Berlin, he was again the victim of a severe fit of depression; he passed two months in his room without seeing anyone and he also seems to have spoken on this occasion, as often before, of suicide; at all events, his letters to his mother caused her great sorrow and she feared that the son's end might be the same as the father's.

Like Rousseau, Comte was subject to psychoses associated with depression, excitement and persecution mania, the first and most severe occurring at the age of 28. It was preceded by digestive disturbances, sleeplessness, gloomy thoughts, and delusions that he was being persecuted; frenzied excitement followed and rendered internment necessary; during the period of convalescence he attempted suicide. Eighteen years later he again developed a delusion accompanied by depression: he believed his life to be

[1] *Curriculum Vitae*, v. Gwinner, p. 161. [2] *Ibid.*, p. 164.

in danger in Paris because the revolutionary party in course of formation would persecute him, and he planned a removal to London.

Fechner suffered for more than three years from severe neurasthenic dejection. He was often tempted to suicide but was held back by the conviction that he would "gain nothing by this sin but rather be obliged to pay in a future life for the sufferings from which he had endeavoured to escape in this one."[1]

Mill suffered at 20 from an access of hypochondria which lasted for over six months. Everything which had previously given him pleasure seemed hollow and indifferent; he was burdened by a feeling which he compared to the Methodist convert's "conviction of sin." He asked himself whether he would be happy if all his ideals for the betterment of the world could be realized on the spot and an irrepressible self-consciousness answered "no." Thereupon his heart sank within him and nothing seemed left to live for. He was not quite incapable of continuing his usual activities but he performed them purely mechanically. "I frequently asked myself if I could, or if I was bound to, go on living, when life must be passed in this manner," he wrote, "and I generally answered to myself that I did not think I could possibly bear it beyond a year."[2]

Stirner, like Spinoza, was one of the people who always seemed calm and equable and who would always be thought unemotional did not their works betray the fact that the

[1] Lasswitz, p. 44.

[2] Mill, p. 140.

calmness was due to self-control and the equability a mask. But we also possess other and very remarkable evidence of the abnormal intensity of his inhibitions. At the age of 30 he applied to the provincial educational authority for a post as teacher; when this was provisionally refused his disappointment was so great that he renounced for ever any further attempt to obtain a post under government. The displeasure-inhibition was therefore of an exceptionally persistent character. In another connexion we find it present in a definitely morbid degree of intensity. He relates that his first wife once unconsciously exposed herself in her sleep; from that moment it was impossible for him ever to seek physical contact with her again. It should be borne in mind that he had been married for hardly nine months when she died and that he had only known her for five years.

Spencer is one of the very few thinkers who were aware of their inhibitions and spoke of them: "Ever since I was a boy (when I was unfortunate in having no brothers or sisters) I have been longing to have my affections called out. I have been in the habit of considering myself but half alive; and I have often said that I hoped to begin to live some day."[1] It must have been very difficult for him, at all events on certain occasions, to make up his mind. Before he could decide whether he should emigrate to New Zealand or not, he resorted to the same device as Schopenhauer—a list of pros and cons—to which, having a mathematical mind,

[1] Spencer I, pp. 478-9.

he allotted marks on Franklin's principle, with the following result :—

	England Advantages		*New Zealand Advantages*
10	Greater domestic comforts	20	More agreeable climate
10	Larger choice of society	40	Better health
20	Excitement in Literature	30	Less anxiety
6	,, in Science	35	More natural and therefore happier occupation
10	,, in Art	30	Eventually more spare time
30	Intercourse with relations	25	Ample provision for old age and better prospect for family
5	Theatres	100	Marriage
8	Music	8	Literature
8	Politics	3	Science
3	Accessibility of Continent	6	Music
		4	Politics[1]
110		301	

It need hardly be said that, in spite of the overwhelming advantages of New Zealand, Spencer stayed at home; in the same way, in spite of the 100 marks for married bliss, he remained single—in practice the inhibitions win the day. Finally, as a severe sufferer from neurasthenia, Spencer was subject to lengthy fits of depression which reduced his capacity for work to a minimum; in the three years during which he was writing his autobiography he did not write more than fifteen lines a day.

Nietzsche was an unusually shy man; the marked contrast between the aggressiveness of his writings and

[1] *Ibid.*, p. 370.

the docility of his personal relations frequently caused comment. Infuriated by the continual noise in his lodging he decided, for the fourth time, to move; he thought out an angry speech, but it became a mild request and he remained. He was furious with his friend Rée; he could not, however, bring himself to dispatch the ten letters which he had written, but re-wrote each of them. Even Basel, he says, made him quite melancholy. Torturing headaches increased his gloom in the ensuing years, he was filled with a longing for death and hoped that an attack of apoplexy would bring him release.

Veiled though they are under the kaleidoscopic mantle of individuality, all these characteristics and trends in the great thinkers assume unmistakable common forms: warning voices and the longing for an outlet for emotions, diffident and gauche behaviour, fear, cautiousness, mistrust, exceptional persistence of inhibitive influences, a tendency to anxiety and depression to the point of harbouring thoughts of suicide—all these are, for us, signs of abnormally strong inhibitions, especially when they are found combined in one individual. Twenty-two out of thirty of the great philosophers exhibit these signs in a more or less sharply-defined form; hence twenty-two out of thirty were men with abnormally intense inhibitions.

We have now completed the first stage in testing the inhibition hypothesis, viz., the production of proof that abnormally intense inhibitions are found in the great thinkers, and indeed are the general rule amongst them. The fundamental assumption of the inhibition hypothesis is therefore shown to be *vera causa.*

We must not be misled by the fact that we have not found signs of excessive inhibition in *all* the great thinkers; traces will be shown later to have existed in Fichte and Hartmann, whilst we know too little of Epicurus, Bacon, Hobbes, Malebranche, Berkeley, and Feuerbach to expect to be able to discover symptoms which are often of an inconspicuous kind. If, therefore, the probability is established that inactivity and inaptitude are due in the case of the great majority of the philosophers to excessive inhibitions, we need not doubt that the same characteristics, due to the same cause, exist in the small minority as well.

The general level of inhibition is higher in the philosophers than in the ordinary run of men, but this higher level is as little constant as the normal one, for in one set of thinkers we find fluctuations of intensity and in another set a continuous increase or decrease.

We must assume that rises and falls are present in the case of the numerous thinkers who were subject to passing fits of depression; during these fits the intensity of inhibition is increased and when they pass it falls again, without, however, necessarily coming back to the previous level.

We observe a slow decline in the intensity of the inhibitions in Hume who, originally too cautious to write about religion at all, gradually overcame his fears to the extent of expressing his views, even though he provided himself with loopholes for escape. The same process manifested itself in Schopenhauer by a gradual decrease in the number of fits of fear.

Other thinkers experienced a slow increase in the

intensity of their inhibitions as life went on. Rousseau, for example, said: "Though I am by nature shy, I was at times bold in my youth, but never in my riper years."[1] And K. Fischer writes of Schelling: "The courage of youth and its fiery self-confidence had declined, and it seems to me that a repugnance towards everything connected with publishing and printing had set in; a mistrust of his own printed word was one of the hidden motives which explain his literary silence whilst still in early manhood."[2]

Our conclusions are then :—

1. The great thinkers are men with more than normally intense inhibitions.

2. With them, as with others, the intensity of the inhibitions may change in the course of life.

[1] Bk. IV (p. 164). [2] VII, p. 32.

CHAPTER XXI

CAN UNSUITABLENESS FOR PRACTICAL LIFE BE EXPLAINED BY THE INHIBITION HYPOTHESIS ?

The inhibition hypothesis is built on the firm foundation of an exceptional intensity of inhibition in the great thinkers. Is it possible to trace the unsuitableness of the philosophers for practical life to the same cause ? This is the second question to be asked in making the test which we have already outlined.[1]

What *is* unsuitableness for practical life ? Our formula would define it thus : unsuitableness equals diffidence plus incapacity. By diffidence we mean, not fear of the practical tasks of life, but the fact that a man, no matter from what motive, avoids action and therefore postpones it for as long as possible, refuses to take opportunities, or misses them, or often either interrupts a task or gives it up altogether—all of which are things contrary to what is normal. Incapacity, on the other hand, is a general name for a number of lines of conduct having the common factor that they lead to failure, *e.g.*, awkwardness, thoughtlessness, tactlessness, and unsociability —all of them developed to the point of abnormality.

We may make it clear in a few words that abnormally intense inhibitions, *i.e.*, exceptionally powerful inhibitive

[1] Cf. p. 137.

factors, will render all practical action difficult for the person in whom they occur; every sensation of shame, fear or disgust and every sensation of displeasure will have an exceptionally strong inhibitive effect. Consequently, whenever such sensations occur—and they occur in every sphere of practical life—he will postpone taking action, let opportunities pass or defer them until too late, interrupt work begun or soon abandon it: in a word he will avoid action where it can possibly be avoided, and be passive and diffident.

But how about incapacity? In so far as it is based on awkwardness—in other words, for the greater part—it may easily be explained, as has been shown above, by exceptionally strong inhibitions; we call an action awkward which has been considerably disturbed or changed in its nature through nervousness and diffidence. Tactlessness, too, which is generally, after all, only a form of social awkwardness, we can understand at once as being based on intense inhibition. Unsociability is a more difficult case: here we must remember that a strongly inhibited person may upon short acquaintance be quite friendly and companionable on account of his diffidence and fear; he may tolerate much that is unpleasant and tedious to him and if challenged may even show patience and refrain from energetic defence. But when enough explosive material has accumulated, some occasion will provoke a furious outburst directed against an astonished colleague, friend or wife. Hence the germ of conflict with the outside world, which is the essence of unsociability, lies in strong inhibition itself and no particularly intense combative instinct need be present.

Even the lack of foresight and the carelessness which the philosophers so often exhibited in matters of money and profession are, paradoxical though it may seem, connected with their inhibitions. Rousseau[1] has described this very graphically: his diffidence and nervousness generally prevented him from doing anything with his money; if he did spend it, it was not without embarrassment, shame and inward resistance, and his only return was trouble and annoyance. Consequently he despised money, did not wish for it when he was without it, and kept it for a long time when he had it because he did not know how to spend it. When, however, a convenient and pleasant opportunity for spending arose the money vanished at once. In this case the intensity of inhibition explains the weakness of the will to earn and, indeed, of the whole money interest.

The inhibitions often interfere in this way with the formation of the professional and pecuniary interests and their development to normal strength, for this development can only take place through action which, in turn, is never completely free from unpleasant experiences; if, however, the latter attain an undue power of inhibition the person concerned will be checked rather than guided by his misadventures and the flow of impulses into the channels where the professional interests are formed will not take place. This does not mean that the deficiency of these interests or the display of carelessness in these matters is to be explained in this way in the case of all thinkers, or that no other factors can come into play; I have merely wished to draw attention to the connexion

[1] Bk. I (p. 47).

between the state of being inhibited and the fact of a lack of interest in practical things—a connexion which undoubtedly existed in many thinkers.

Unfitness for practical affairs, in itself a product of inhibition, has in turn, as has several times been emphasized, the effect of aggravating the tendency towards inactivity, since failures give rise to the fear of making new attempts.

Thus the inhibition hypothesis is capable of explaining unsuitableness for the practical affairs of life in all its components. It can go further: this unsuitableness is, as we have seen, to be found in all great thinkers, though in very different degrees; if it is based on intense inhibition, *i.e.*, a quantitative factor, we necessarily expect such differences, for the degree of inhibition is naturally also capable of varying considerably and according as it is very high or approaching normal the unsuitableness will be found more or less pronounced.

And, finally, the changes in the extent of practical unsuitableness, its rises and falls and its constant movement in one or the other direction in the course of a lifetime, may, without forcing the argument, be attributed to the analogous changes in the intensity of inhibition which we have just considered.

Thus the variations in the level of the intensity of inhibition, together with its gradual movement throughout life, lead to the consequence that the practical life of great thinkers is a kaleidoscope in which lesser and greater degrees of unsuitableness, its application to all or its restriction to a few aspects of life, its rises and falls, and its gradual increase or decrease, are one by one presented to view. Hence it comes that in describing practical unsuitableness it has so often been necessary to make exceptions—to say that "nearly all," "most," "the majority," "the great majority," or even "many" of the great thinkers showed passivity and incapacity in such or such a matter, but never "all" or "without exception"; hence it was also necessary to insist that the expressions "passivity" and "incapacity" only mean a reduction and not a complete absence of activity and capacity.

We have thus taken the second step in testing the inhibition hypothesis and may now say: the hypothesis of inhibition is admirably calculated to explain in all its components the phenomenon of unsuitableness for the practical affairs of life.

CHAPTER XXII

POETRY AND RELIGION

The inhibition hypothesis is able to explain the phenomenon of unsuitableness for the practical affairs of life; so also is the predominance hypothesis. Which, then, is right? Our answer must be based upon the reliability of the fundamental assumptions and also upon the extent to which we are enabled to explain known facts or even to discover new ones.

The predominance hypothesis is based on the assumption that philosophic interest is more intense than all other human interests; we only know for certain, however, that in many philosophers it is greater than the pecuniary interest: the generalization remains, as we have seen, uncertain. The inhibition hypothesis is based on the assumption that the inhibitive factors are abnormally effective in the philosophers, and to a large extent this assumption has been verified. In so far as these considerations are concerned, therefore, preference must be given to the inhibition hypothesis.

It remains to explain the further phenomena of the philosophers' psychology: where are these phenomena? We have none on hand, but a good hypothesis is essentially one which renders possible the discovery of fresh material. Let us then see whither the predominance hypothesis will lead us.

If in a given individual the philosophic interest far exceeds all others in intensity, he will feel powerfully the need to give it plenty of room for exercise. If, like the great thinkers, he is able to do this, it is not easy to see what else he is to do or what else can happen to him except, of course, that, in accordance with the predominance theory, he will be unsuitable for the practical things of life. Thus the predominance hypothesis does not lead us to fresh facts.

The inhibition hypothesis, however, does. If an individual is unable to give full rein to his impulses owing to the presence of inhibitive factors, so that the practical interests are in part incompletely formed and in part inadequately exercised, the impulses will, as it were, open a safety-valve, will seek an alternative activity and satisfaction: this, in the philosopher, is philosophic thought. But it might well be the case that this activity, for all its persistence and intensity, fails to supply a complete outlet for the pent-up impulses and that the energies thus deprived of a normal means of discharge are forced to seek yet other channels. Freud teaches that sex-impulses deprived of their normal channel of satisfaction can be diverted from their original aim into socially valuable forms of activity. This process he calls sublimation. Sublimation is, however, by no means restricted, as Freud thought, to the sexual impulses; we have seen that the impulse to go on living and to secure requital gives rise to the belief in immortality and that the impulse to seek safety creates belief in God. And when the combative instinct finds expression in polemical writings, revenge in satire, and the love of children in care that literary works shall be made available for posterity, we have the sublimation of non-sexual impulses. Sublimated impulses may be turned into scientific, artistic, religious, or social work. Social work involves action and is not to be sought among the philosophers; we must, however, find out whether they followed artistic and religious pursuits.

We must look for pursuits rather than for talent—at least we have no ground for expecting to find such talent amongst the philosophers: if some of them had a gift for poetry, that is a fact which stands by itself, and one which is by no means essential to the endeavour to create forms of art, being merely a requisite to their having æsthetic value.

Our interest, however, is not in the æsthetic but only in the psychological side of the question; we regard the poetic productions of many thinkers—including numerous untalented ones—solely as evidence that they were intensely inhibited people who had such powerful impulses to cope with that they could not all be kept to the highway of philosophic thought, and some straggled into the by-ways of poetry in spite of the roughness of the track.

In the *Phaedo* we are told that Socrates, when in prison, began to write poetry—a thing far from his mind until that time. His first work was a hymn to Apollo, but the lack of inspiration thereafter caused him to content himself with rendering a number of Æsop's fables into verse.

Plato wrote dramatic works as a young man and burned them later; some of his philosophic works are, nevertheless, poems, and poems of immense power and beauty. Plato is the great poet amongst the philosophers.

Aristotle cannot claim fame as a poet but he wrote verse—*inter alia*, an elegy on the death of a friend.

St Augustine, on the other hand, had great poetic talent and many passages of the *Confessions* are also, from the purely æsthetic point of view, of great emotional power.

Bruno wrote a whole series of poems, songs, satires, and comedies, and his philosophic work also, like that of Plato, is full of poetic rhythm.

Leibniz was no poet, it is true, but even he expressed in a philosophic poem his sorrow at the death of the Queen of Prussia.

Berkeley attempted to obtain support for his scheme to found a college in the Bermudas by publishing lively verse in favour of it.

Rousseau, again, was a philosopher who may be counted amongst the poets; he wrote dramas, short stories and novels, some of which were of great artistic value.

Though he refused the professorship of literature, Kant, nevertheless, wrote verses; Borowski,[1] it is true, suggests that they were quite trivial occasional poems contributed to pamphlets commemorating professors who had died, but Jachmann finds Kant's verses full of deep thought and powerful in their expression.

Fichte, also, had poetic gifts which find effective expression, for example, in *Die Bestimmung des Menschen*. He also wrote numerous short poems.

[1] p. 78.

As a young man Hegel wrote a pantheistic hymn and as a man of mature years he again made some attempt at verse on the occasion of his betrothal.

Schelling wrote a number of poems which show unmistakable rhythm and facility of expression.

In many passages of his philosophic works Schopenhauer shows himself to be a poet of considerable creative power. This is so true that his chief work has been called a metaphysical novel. He also published a number of verses, though he himself did not attach poetical value to them.

Apart from his satires on medicine and natural philosophy, Fechner also published a volume of lyric poems and a *Little Book of Riddles*, all showing much imagination and originality, though too abstractly written for poetry. In youth, he tended more towards art than science, but even then he admitted that he lacked the " inner essentials "[1] for artistic productivity.

Spencer, too, experimented with verse at the age of 23 and set his hand to a poem, " The Angel of Truth," and a drama, " The Rebel."

Nietzsche, like Plato, St Augustine, Bruno and Rousseau, is one of the philosophers who had not only the impulse but also the talent to create poetic form and thereby demonstrate that Schopenhauer was wrong in thinking that a man could not be both a philosopher and a poet. " Zarathustra," both in content and in form, must be classed with the greatest poetry in the world's literature and a number of his smaller poems have great and unique charm, many indeed being of enchanting beauty.

[1] Lasswitz, p. 39.

Finally, Hartmann, also, published a volume of "Dramatic Poems."

Thus, more than half of the great philosophers wrote some poetry, even though generally not much—an astonishing confirmation of our hypothesis that the same psychical structure, namely, intense inhibition of the impulses to action, is at the base of both philosophic and poetic creation.

That religious sentiment is also due to the sublimation of impulses to action had already been perceived by Rousseau, for Julie says in the *Nouvelle Héloïse* that devotion to everything of which she was fond could not entirely fill her heart. Her heart had other powers, which *were not used and which it could not use.* And because her soul could not satisfy its longings in this world, it elevated itself to the fount of all sensation and all existence.

Religious interest is unmistakable in nearly all our philosophers, and in many of them it is revealed under a particularly impressive form. We shall seek in vain amongst them, it is true, for founders or reformers of religions, for their lack of activity and of practical sense militated against them in this field as much as in that of politics; moreover, only one of them, St Augustine, would have had the requisite religious genius. There is only one founder of a sect, Comte, and there are only two priests, Malebranche and Berkeley, among them. In the case of all the others—and, apart from Stirner, they all dealt with religious problems—religious interest only came into operation when it influenced the choice of problems, *i.e.*, when it merged with the desire for knowledge and thus became a component of philosophic interest.

Although, then, the religious interest of the great philosophers finds its outlet almost exclusively in their normal pursuit of philosophy, even this veiled form of activity furnishes us with evidence that it is an active interest, and this again is proof of the intense inhibitions of the philosophers, since religious interest, as we have seen, must also be regarded as a result of the sublimation of impulses to action: and, the more active it is, the stronger, we must conclude, are the inhibitions which divert the impulses to action from their original goal.

In sum—the facts that more than half of the philosophers wrote poetry and that nearly all devoted thought to the problems of religious philosophy furnish confirmation of the inhibition hypothesis.

CHAPTER XXIII

NEUROSES

The ability to sublimate impulses is, as we know from psychoanalysis, one which varies in degree but is never unlimited; a part of the impulse-energies can be set in operation only by means of actions directed towards the original goal and satisfied by its attainment. When insurmountable inhibitions prevent the unsublimated impulse-energies from completely reaching their goal, neurotic ailments set in. Intense inhibitions, therefore, constitute a predisposition to neurosis. If, at the same time, the subject of the intense inhibitions is a person with strong impulses, residuary partial impulses which have found no outlet in action are the more likely to remain. Intensity of impulse, as Freud also emphasizes, carries with it a predisposition to neurosis. The philosophers, we know, are men with strong impulses; again, the inhibition hypothesis assumes that they are also men with intense inhibitions; consequently we should expect them to be especially predisposed to neuroses, to be subject to neurasthenia, hypochondria, depression, hysteria, and to fits of fear and obsession: moreover, if it is true that delusions may also spring from this source, we shall hardly fail to find the pathological conditions associated with mental disorder.

We have already seen that a quite remarkably large number of our thinkers suffered from attacks of depression. What I described by that name in a previous chapter is in the case of some of them not definitely pathological; others are border cases, but the majority are typical of an unmistakably diseased condition, the other characteristics of which were not relevant to our earlier study but are the more so now.

Whilst still in his early thirties St Augustine began to feel the inner change; he was still chained to the world but the new will, the longing for God, was beginning to assert itself in him: "Thus with the baggage of the present world was I as sweetly overladen, as a man uses to be in a dream," he says in the *Confessions*, "and those thoughts with which I meditated upon thee were like the struggles of such as would get up; who being yet overcome with a deep sleep, fall again into it."[1] Then anxiety began to assert itself in his soul; his daily tasks became a torture to him, he continually implored God to rescue him and whenever he could he sought refuge from the world in church. His torment of soul became ever more insupportable, his professional duties ever more burdensome, and his longing for delivery ever more passionate. We recognize in his poetic and religious descriptions the symptoms of anxiety-neurosis—depression, aversion from effort, dissatisfaction with the life he had previously led, and fear. A small cause—the story of the sudden conversion of two officials—served to release the pent-up energies: a powerful emotional storm shook his being, he was seized with terrible remorse of

[1] p. 427.

conscience for his apathy, he tore his hair, beat his forehead and shed floods of tears, until at last, whilst reading a passage in the Bible which he regarded as a message from God, inward peace came over him and promised him that he should be healed if he would renounce the world—or, to express it in medical terms, the inhibited impulses were led to sublimation and an outlet for activity was thereby afforded them.

The remarkable neurosis which the young Descartes developed in the winter camp on the Danube has already engaged our attention; it was characterized by unrest, depression, excitement, despair and alarming dreams and was unquestionably a complex of neurasthenic symptoms. The cure occurred with similar swiftness to St Augustine's, through a sudden inspiration—the discovery of analytical geometry and the resultant decision to base philosophy upon the same reliable principles and methods as had proved so fruitful in mathematics.

At the age of 18, Hume fell sick of exhaustion, inertia, and depression after severe mental overwork; he felt himself greatly impeded in his work through being no longer able to concentrate or to link up his thoughts consistently, owing to the necessity for continually interrupting them in order to do other things for the sake of relief. He was able, it is true, in the following years to conceive a large number of philosophic ideas and to sketch their outlines roughly in writing, but when he wished to define, co-ordinate, and expound them, he found to his great sorrow that his powers had failed him. For four years he fought his neurasthenic fatigue, at times by resting and at others by studying, but both proved equally bad: on the other hand, activity and change did him good, and he decided to adopt a practical career and become a business man. After two months, however, he gave up the attempt as hopeless and undertook journeys which at last brought him the wished-for cure.

Rousseau, a man whose sex-life was coloured by masochistic and exhibitionist tendencies, who showed ethical deficiencies and was inclined to vagabondage—who was, in a word, a definite psychopath—was seized at 24 by a neurosis of neurasthenic and hypochondriacal type. He became enervated and dejected, wept over the most trivial things and believed himself on the verge of death. After a transient improvement he fell a victim, through a slight physical strain, to a curious attack characterized by loud hammering at the temples and by a buzzing, murmuring, whistling and knocking in the ears, accompanied by sudden deafness; the noises in the ears and the deafness continued from that day onwards, and shortness of breath, sleeplessness, anxiety and moodiness also ensued, whilst vertigo on bending down, and lack of breath when walking or lifting weights made all physical activity impossible for him. Finally, he conceived the hypochondriacal idea that he was suffering from a polypus of the heart and he set out on a journey to Montpellier to consult a famous doctor there. On the way, however, he made the acquaintance of a lady who showed interest in him—" and then good-bye to poor Jean-Jacques, or rather to fever, vapours and polypus—all vanished in her presence, save some few palpitations of which she would not cure me."[1] When he had passed his fifties

[1] Bk. VI (p. 31).

the unfortunate man, unfitted to face life, crushed by pecuniary worries, and persecuted by governments, slowly fell a victim to mental disease. At the same time as *Émile*, *i.e.*, in 1762, there was published by a Geneva physician a work on education which was awarded a prize by the Haarlem Academy. Rousseau conceived the notion that this book, apart from a few platitudes, was copied word for word from the first volume of *Émile*—a completely baseless idea. He believed that he had been mysteriously robbed and said that the award of a prize and even the Haarlem Academy itself were frauds invented to conceal the theft from the public. Early in 1766 he arrived in England, where Hume had offered the harassed thinker safe shelter in the rustic surroundings of which he was so fond. When, however, the English newspapers which had at first proclaimed his fame began to mock him and thus appeared to him in the light of hateful calumniatory sheets, insanity broke out in its full force. Rousseau suddenly fled, leaving behind him a letter in which he accused Hume and his landlord of being involved in a conspiracy to humiliate and dishonour him. He wandered about England and wrote to the Lord Chancellor that he wanted to leave the country, but for fear of his enemies, did not dare to leave his house; he therefore requested to be supplied with an official guard. In a letter to General Conway he asserted that Hume had made him a prisoner of state, expressed the fear that he would be murdered and petitioned to be allowed to leave England. He did in fact return to France in the summer of 1767. Here, however, he also failed to find peace; in the *château* of the Prince de Conti, who treated him with the greatest respect and kindness, he again saw in every one an enemy and a party to the great conspiracy against him. A friend fell ill; Rousseau believed that he was accused of poisoning him: the steward of the *château* died; Rousseau was convinced that he was regarded as a murderer and asked that a post-mortem examination should be held. A year later, he left the *château*, again wandered about for months and, early in 1769 accepted an invitation to a *château* near Bourgoin. "The floor on which I stand has eyes, the walls have ears," is how he describes his condition—the typical persecution-mania associated with paranoia—"Surrounded by spies and ever-watchful attendants who wish me harm, I dash down, ill at ease and unable to concentrate, a few hurried and disconnected words on paper, but from lack of time I can hardly read them over, still less revise them."[1] His delusions became more and more absurd; at one moment he believed himself involved in an attack on the life of Louis XIV, and at another he accused his enemies of giving him colourless ink so as to make it impossible for him to write his *Confessions*.

In his early years, Kant suffered from tightness of the chest, accompanied by depression bordering on disgust for life. Through self-discipline and especially by diverting his attention, he slowly learned to counteract the effects of this condition upon his moods, thoughts and actions, though the tightness itself continued.

Schelling complained continually of fits of a "hypochondriacal mood" which increased, he said, in the

[1] *Confessions, 2nd Part,* Vol. IV, p. 7.

course of many years; he lacked his former freshness and enterprise; his ability to work and self-confidence diminished; and insuperable diffidence in preparing and publishing his works set in—all characteristic symptoms of neurasthenia.

Herbart suffered from the same disease as a young student: its symptoms were despair, depression, and ideas of suicide.

Schopenhauer went through a series of illnesses at 35, amongst which he includes "nervous trouble." "I recovered a month ago," he wrote in May 1824 to Osann, "but my nerves are still so weak that I have not been able to answer your letter earlier owing to the trembling of my hands and I only do it now with great difficulty. I drag myself about and fall asleep in the day-time."[1] Eight years later he again fell ill; we do not know whether it was a physical sickness, but in any case it was associated with definite nervous symptoms: he shut himself off from all intercourse for two months and fell into such a state of dejection that his mother wrote: "What you tell me about your health, your dislike of seeing people and your gloom worries me more than I can or dare say. You know why."[2]

Comte in his twenty-ninth year suffered from an acute attack of mental disease. We have seen the symptoms already—digestive disturbance, sleeplessness, melancholy delusions of persecution, and in addition fits of excitement and outbreaks of temper so intense as to oblige his wife to leave the house. An enforced stay with and treatment by the famous Esquirol failed to bring about

[1] Ebstein, p. 25.

[2] v. Gwinner, p. 241.

an improvement and it was not until two years later that home treatment led to a slow recovery. In his later years slight but unmistakable symptoms of paranoia developed; the notion that the coming revolutionary party had designs upon his life bears the stamp of persecution-mania as does his self-appointed rôle of High Priest of Mankind that of megalomania.

Fechner passed three years of his life in an advanced neurotic condition. The illness began with the signs of neurasthenia—bad sleep, enervation associated with complete inability to think, dejected moods and disgust with life itself. Later a growing fear of the light set in and soon made it impossible for him to read and write, forcing him also to wear a bandage over his eyes when he went out. Finally, he was no longer able to eat or drink and he starved for several weeks until he was reduced to skin and bone. He thought himself lost until one day a woman acquaintance brought him a dish which she had prepared herself and which she had dreamt would be acceptable to him. Fechner did in fact eat it without harm to himself and, from that day, his digestion and general strength, at all events, improved. Not so, however, his eyesight and his ability to perform mental work; on the contrary, a new obsession was added to the neurasthenic and hysterical symptoms already present. "One of the chief symptoms of my mental weakness was that my will was no longer able to control the course of my thoughts. If any object attracted my attention, my thoughts began to turn round and round it, came back to it and bored and entrenched themselves, as it were, in my brain so that I had a clear feeling that my mind was hopelessly lost if I failed to exert every effort of resistance. Often the most trivial things would force themselves upon me in this way and it frequently cost me hours and even days of work to rid my mind of them."[1] The turning point came quite unexpectedly; his fear of the light diminished and after more than three years' existence all symptoms of disease disappeared. As a result of this surprising cure Fechner fell into a "curiously overstrung condition of mind" in which he believed himself called upon by God to perform extraordinary tasks, for which his sufferings were a preparation. He also believed himself to possess exceptional physical and psychical powers. "Evidently," he adds, "my condition was approaching that of mental derangement, but the balance was gradually restored."[2]

Mill's neurasthenic attack has already been described, but its symptoms may be recalled, viz., general indifference and dejection. It lasted for about six months, recurred several times in lesser degree for varying periods—at times for more than a month—and was finally completely overcome.

Spencer was less fortunate. He fell ill at 35 with insomnia and an unpleasant sensation of numbness in the head. In spite of immediate attention the trouble did not cease and Spencer was upset by the least mental strain. Even eighteen months of inactivity could not serve to restore his health, which he never fully regained. He was able at most to do three hours' intensive work daily and though he frequently refrained from doing any at all his neurasthenia continually became worse. At the

[1] Lasswitz, p. 43.

[2] *Ibid.*, p. 46.

end of his sixties he was in an extremely bad state and suffered from long periods of depression which reduced his ability to work to a minimum.

Nietzsche suffered from severe attacks of headache, accompanied by vomiting and eye trouble which obliged him at the early age of 35 to give up his profession of university lecturer, and gravely affected both his capacity for work and his outlook. It is, however, not definitely ascertainable whether his condition was a nervous one, connected possibly with his mind, or whether organic complications had already arisen to account for it.

What Lombroso has exaggeratedly described as the connexion between genius and madness and what Birnbaum diagnoses as the "unexpectedly widespread occurrence of slight psychopathic symptoms"[1] in prominent men comes to light in a particularly striking way among the philosophers. Nearly half of them show not merely psychopathic symptoms but definite neuroses of more or less severe intensity, a few cases terminating in mental derangement; a fact which does not surprise us, because the hypothesis of inhibition had already led us to expect it, and which gives further powerful support to that hypothesis.

The conflict between the predominance hypothesis and that of inhibition is thus decided in the latter's favour. It is established on firmer ground, is equally useful in explaining unsuitableness for practical life, and is superior in heuristic value. Consequently it definitely deserves to be given the preference.

[1] p. 98.

CHAPTER XXIV

PHILOSOPHER AND ARTIST

We have come a long way in order to arrive at an understanding of unsuitableness for practical life, but the journey was worth while for we have found more than we sought—not only understanding, but also new light on the mental life of the great thinkers. Let us summarize what we know of it.

1 The philosophers were men of unusually strong impulses;

2. Their inhibitions were more than normally intense;

3. They showed unsuitableness for practical life;

4. They tended to poetical expression;

5. They were predisposed to neuroses.

We know that unsuitableness for practical life is a result of intense inhibition and that poetic, religious and, if one may say so, neurotic productivity is also a consequence of intense inhibition combined with unusual strength of impulse. Hence, strength of impulse and intensity of inhibition are left as the independent marks of the great thinkers.

The frequency with which they occur leads us to conclude that these conditions are prerequisite to the formation of a great philosopher and we are further led to inquire whether they are also sufficient in themselves. Must a person with powerful impulses and intense inhibitions necessarily become a great thinker or are other paths of mental development also open to him? There is no doubt, as we have seen, that sublimated impulses become springs of artistic and religious creation and, where the power to sublimate is absent, sources of neurotic production; thus a man of strong impulses and intense inhibitions can also be an artist, a religious reformer, the founder of a sect, or a neurotic. Why then does he become a philosopher first and foremost and these other things either not at all or only subsidiarily? Philosophizing is scientific thinking, but in all scientific thinking, and especially in productive scientific thought, invention—that is to say mediative thinking—plays, as we have already seen, a decisive part, for every new discovery and every new proof can only be found by means of such thinking. For discovery, however, intelligence is necessary: indeed, intelligence is essentially and pre-eminently the capacity for discovery. Consequently, anyone who, like the great philosophers, employs inventive thought with conspicuous success, must possess a high degree of intelligence. It is unnecessary to seek chapter and verse to prove the existence of this pre-eminent intelligence in the great philosophers or to relate how one or the other of them was conspicuous as a child for surpassing intellectual gifts or aroused general admiration as a youth for independence of thought, keenness in argument, or the ability to solve difficult tasks. It is sufficient to point to the works of the great thinkers as evidence of their outstanding intelligence. The possession of a higher intelligence than the normal is thus a further condition which must be fulfilled in order that a person may become a great thinker.

But we also ascribe outstanding intelligence to the great poets. It would therefore seem that this fresh factor alone does not complete the complex of conditions requisite to the making of a great thinker.

We have already[1] analysed intelligence and found it to be the capacity for experimenting with thoughts, rejecting useless ones and selecting useful ones. We remember the boy who wished to obtain a flower which he saw behind a fence: numerous ideas occurred to him as to how he might get it. He rejected some and then he found one which seemed useful and he decided to carry it out. We can distinguish three things in such an act of intelligent thought: the basic volition—reducible to impulses—the occurrence of ideas, and their acceptance or rejection. Thus, in ordinary language, the essentials to an act of intelligence are impulse, imagination, and criticism. None of the three factors can be dispensed with: without impulse the imagination would not be exercised, without imagination the impulse would be exhausted in blind and monotonous attempts, and without criticism even the most useless ideas would be accepted and put to the test. In no case would the result be reflexion, invention, or intelligent thought.

Exceptional intelligence therefore postulates an especial development of the three factors: high intensity of impulse, vivid imagination and keen criticism. The pre-

[1] pp. 29 ff.

dominance of either imagination or criticism, then, gives intelligence a further and characteristic stamp.

Let us consider. Philosophizing is scientific thinking, scientific thinking is critical thinking: therefore anyone who, like a great philosopher, successfully manipulates scientific thought must be a keen critic. The artist or the poet has far less need of this, and thus the intelligence of the philosopher is distinguished from that of the artist by the preponderance of the critical factor. It is scientific, that is to say critical intelligence.

There is another factor which especially fits the philosopher for scientific thought, viz., his tendency and ability to co-ordinate:[1] its systematic character is indeed the second indispensable mark of scientific thinking. To co-ordinate means to bring coherence and order into thoughts or observed facts. This impulse towards order, which is common to the philosopher and the paranoic, constitutes a second difference between philosopher and poet, for the poet lacks it and another mechanism is strongly developed in its place—the mechanism of projection. By this we understand the inevitable tendency[2] to look upon psychical processes as things or attributes of the outer world—the tendency which every one exhibits in his very recognition of a real outer world, or again in dreaming about the world of imagination, which he colours rosy or grey; the tendency, again, which explains, as we see in the study of ethno-psychology, why men create demons and gods and which leads the mentally deranged to form hallucinations or distorted ideas of the

[1] Cf. Spencer's remarks on the architectonic instinct, II, pp. 450 f.

[2] See Hoche, p. 966.

world. These cases represent, however, only the extremes, the final limits, as it were, of projection, in so far as belief in the reality of the projected contents as external things is actually present. Intermediate are the capacity and the obligation to personify and dramatize thoughts and impulses, without absolutely believing in the objective reality of the creations of the imagination—a connecting link again between paranoic and poet. When developed in a specific direction—that of what is called creative power—it is a quite essential factor of poetic talent and indeed its actual basis. We thus find the mechanism of projection unmistakably at work in those philosophers who were also poets: Plato's and Bruno's *Dialogues* are dramatized philosophy, Rousseau's *Émile* is a philosophic novel and Nietzsche's *Zarathustra* is also a wonderfully clear example of the personification of philosophic teaching. In general, however, the projective mechanism is not greatly developed in the philosophers; their poetry is, on this very account, lifeless and abstract. Without the capacity for projection, no poetic talent can find expression. Even those philosophers whom we have named as having some significance as poets—Plato, Bruno, Rousseau, and Nietzsche—by no means exhibit a highly-developed capacity for projection; what they produce is dramatized philosophy, it is true, but not philosophic dramas such as *Faust*. Their poetic powers lie—as in the case of St Augustine, Fichte, Schelling, Schopenhauer, Fechner, and Stirner—more in the field of form and language. We cannot therefore state that this difference between philosopher and poet resides in the fact that the philosopher, as opposed to the poet, has no poetic talent—

for this talent is a composite one of which the one, formal, factor of literary ability may be present in the philosopher, whereas the other, material, factor of projective capacity is never present to any great extent and is generally completely absent. The difference is therefore that, whereas in the philosopher the mechanism of co-ordination is hypertrophic and the mechanism of projection little developed, the situation is reversed in the poet. That the mechanism of projection is also active in painters and sculptors as a component of their talents is obvious from the very nature of these forms of art, which create an inward impulse towards pictorial and plastic expression. Without it the creations of their imagination would have no life of their own and no objectivity: it is projection that makes them stand out as independent, figures like dream-forms in the eye of the artist, who thereupon endeavours to recreate them in his material. Whether the mechanism of projection plays a part in the musician also, I am unable to say.

Apart from this, the preponderance of the critical factor in his intelligence and the predominance of the mechanism of co-ordination are the characteristics which distinguish the philosopher from the artist.

CHAPTER XXV

PHILOSOPHER, MAN OF RELIGION, NEUROTIC

THE mere fact that a man of strong impulse is cut off from active participation in the affairs of life does not of itself justify any expectation of artistic or philosophic productivity. It may be that no god will give him the means of saying what he suffers and that he is consequently without either artistic or philosophic means of expression. There still remains, however, the religious life, either as a reformer, a founder of a sect or an ardent devotee of mystic experience. This presupposes the presence of what the philosopher lacks—a high degree of submission to authority. The psychoanalyst would call this a strong positive father-complex, but I should prefer to regard it as an exceptionally intense form of a primitive impulse—the instinct of submission. Even the most revolutionary reformers or founders of religions exhibit this submission in the form of the recognition and acceptance of divine authority. Buddha shows it least of all, and his religion on that very account may be as well or better called philosophy, for the philosophers, unlike men of religion, are nearly all opponents of authority, people with a negative father-complex, to use the psychoanalytical phrase again, rebels against the instinct of submission and energetic enemies of its consequences in politics, morals, philosophy, and religion. Even where they outwardly conform to religious opinions, it is often only for the sake of appearances, as in the case of Plato, Hobbes, and Hume. Epicurus, Bruno, Spinoza, Schopenhauer, Comte, Feuerbach, Stirner, Spencer, Hartmann, and Nietzsche, however, quite frankly "philosophized with the sledge-hammer." Socrates attacked the authority of pseudo-learning and Bacon that of scholasticism. Rousseau was an intellectual revolutionary and nearly all the others were revolutionaries in the field of philosophy, not only creating new ideas but making every effort to upset the existing ones—not, like the founders of religions, in order to set up a new authority in place of the old, but in order to establish their own intellectual sway over the ruins. Jaspers says, much to the point: "As opposed to the mythic-daemonic world-order, the philosophic order is characterized by not resting on authority, on mere acceptance, on belief and on hearsay, but it appeals to the individual views gained by men in the course of their own experiences."[1]

We are entitled to assume from the keen religious interest shown by most of the philosophers that the reason for these revolutionary tendencies is to be sought not in the weakness of the submissive instinct but in the formation of powerful reactions against it. Thus in the religious man, it is the submissive instinct which is strongest, whilst in the philosopher the revolutionary tendencies have the upper hand.

When, however, a person with neither artistic nor philosophic means of expression finds his way to the

[1] p. 173.

religious life blocked because his submissive instinct is too little developed or because, perhaps, some other and unknown hindrances exist, he inevitably draws near to the god with the Janus head—neurosis. For neurosis, though it provides an outlet for the pent-up impulse-energies, has its outcome in torment instead of satisfaction. Even the highest artistic talent, however, and even the greatest religious or philosophic gifts cannot always offer a shield from neurosis. Hölderlin, C. F. Meyer, Luther, St Augustine, Rousseau, Comte, and many other philosophers demonstrate this with unmistakable clearness. Strong inhibitions are necessary in order that the impulses shall not find their main outlet in action. Talent, even though it is not indispensable, greatly favours their transformation into artistic, religious, or philosophic production, but in order that they shall really be transformed into such production and not stray into the *via dolorosa* of neurosis another thing is necessary—what we called, adopting Freud's name for it, the capacity for sublimation and understood to mean the ability to divert impulses from their original goal towards other and socially valuable activities. This ability must be developed to a noteworthy degree in an intellectually productive person.

We have already seen that this capacity for sublimation is always restricted and that never more than a part of the impulse-energies can be sublimated. We also know that it is subject to variations in the course of a lifetime. It is such variations towards the negative side—sudden drops in the capacity for sublimating—that bring about acute neuroses in the great thinkers. Increases, on the other hand, lead to the cure of such illnesses and the sudden reappearance, or considerable increase, of productivity, as in the case of St Augustine, Descartes, and Fechner.

We have no certain knowledge of the causes of these variations: physical illness may play a part in harming the capacity for sublimation, as may possibly also failures and overwork. We do, however, want to know what this mysterious capacity really is in itself, how we obtain it, and what determines its full development.

We have already seen[1] that impulses may be transferred from end to means and from one action to a similar one: it is in this way that all our diverted interests come into existence. If, in consequence, artistic or scientific work, let us say, is performed in order to satisfy an ambition, the impulse will be transferred to this satisfaction: it is frequently observed that a woman with an erotic interest in a man transfers it to his intellectual, political, and social activities. The new interest may then become fairly, or indeed entirely, independent and may thus continue even after the original purpose of ambition or love has ceased to hold good; it is in such cases especially, the social value of the new interest being an *a priori* condition, that we speak of sublimation. If, in addition, the unsatisfied love for a man is transformed into love of God—*i.e.*, an erotic emotion into a religious one—or if the combative impulse becomes a component of surgical interest, we have to deal with the transfer of impulses from their original activity to a similar one, and this process we shall also term "sublimation" in view of

[1] pp. 94 ff.

the independence and the social value of the new interest acquired. Sublimation is thus nothing more than a special case of the general transference from end to means, or from one form of activity to another and similar one, characterized by social value and independence.

On what does the high degree of development of this capacity in the great thinkers depend? The most obvious assumption is that a more than normal amount of inhibition in itself calls forth a high capacity for sublimation, since as a result of the inhibition an enormous amount of impulse energy is thwarted of its original destination and thus forced into some other path, with the result that, as it were, a continuous exercise of the capacity for transfer takes place. This is probably true to some extent but the question then arises: Why are these impulse energies transformed in one person mainly into artistic or philosophic and in another into neurotic activities (if we may use the expression)? In answer, we must again point to the talent which the one possesses and the other does not and which causes the artistic or philosophic work of the one to cause satisfaction, whereas similar endeavours by the other leave him unsatisfied and therefore dissuade him from renewing them. As a result, we should expect a further exercise of the sublimation faculty of the talented person and its neglect in the untalented one. But we still do not know what caused the neuroses of the great artists and thinkers, many of whom, like Rousseau and Spencer, suffered in varying degrees throughout their whole lives. Factors which are still unknown must play a part, determining by their presence the degree of the sublimative capacity. They must, it would seem, be able to effect its temporary or lasting diminution, or even complete suppression, although inhibition is strong and talent unusually high.

Our analysis of the sublimative capacity ends here in uncertainty. We must be content to say: highly developed capacity for sublimation distinguishes the artist, the philosopher and the man of religion from the neurotic.

CHAPTER XXVI

PHILOSOPHER AND SCIENTIST: ORIGINALITY

Have we now reconstructed the philosopher? Does a man with strong impulses, intense inhibitions, and high capacity for sublimation, whose critical intelligence and love of system predominate over his projective mechanism and in whom strong revolutionary tendencies outweigh his submissive instinct, necessarily become a thinker? He will not become a practical man, for his inhibitions are too strong, or an artist, for his projective power is too weak: he is protected from wasting his impulse energies in neurosis by his high capacity for sublimation, whilst his critical intelligence and love of system direct him towards scientific thought. Thus, he will become a scholar—but why a philosopher? Doubtless the degree of inhibition plays a part: many other branches of knowledge call for more activity than does philosophy; they call for experiment or at least for observation—in any case for action; and action, when a certain degree of inhibition has been attained, arouses antipathies which are only overcome with difficulty. Secondly, importance attaches to the specialized interest which the historian, mathematician, botanist, or astronomer brings to bear, whilst in the philosopher it is completely eclipsed by the specifically philosophic interest. We have already seen that this philosophic interest is a product of the merging of the desire for knowledge with the impulses to action, and at this point I ought perhaps to explain in what way specialized interest in a particular branch of knowledge, such as history, mathematics, or astronomy, differs from it. This, however, I can only do to a very slight extent by saying that this specialized interest is in many people compounded of theoretical interest and a specific practical one—*e.g.*, the interest in botany of theoretical plus agricultural, or the interest in mathematics of theoretical plus architectural interest. In other people, again, its development is due to complicated and entirely individual processes: interest in astronomy may be fostered by religious feelings or that in zoology by the instinct to care for children. These remain, however, individual cases which have no general bearing, and I am not prepared to make a general statement at this point. In the philosophers, at all events, the specialized interests are outweighed by the philosophic interest or, when strongly developed, they are derived from it.

We have thus laid down, or if that be impossible, at all events indicated, the conditions which are requisite, and adequate, in order that a man may become a philosopher. But do they suffice to produce a thinker of the stamp of the *great* philosophers whose lives have provided us with the raw material for our researches? It might be thought that this was purely a question of quantity and that a matter of more or less strength of impulse, inhibition, intelligence, co-ordination, independence or capacity for sublimation might be decisive as to the greatness of a philosopher. There is some truth in this, for the greatness of a thinker is determined by the combination of originality with the power to influence the mind of his time: in developing an original thought, however, in bringing evidence in its support and in following up its consequences—and on these things the power to influence contemporary thought largely depends—all the above-mentioned factors play their part. But are they enough to produce original thought itself? Do they give a man that mysterious creative power which enables him to wander far from the beaten path, audaciously adding new associations of ideas to mankind's treasury of thought—do they give him that originality which is the outstanding mark of genius?

We know originality to be not only a mark of the great philosophers but equally a characteristic of the great physicists and mathematicians—indeed of all workers in the specialized fields of knowledge. It is found in poets, painters, sculptors, engineers, politicians and business men; indeed, even in the case of neurotics and the mentally diseased the distinction between ordinary people and "originals" does not cease to hold good. Originality is thus independent of abnormal inhibitions, for otherwise practical men would not have it: nor can it depend upon a special development of the capacity for sublimation, otherwise neurotics would lack it; nor again upon a predominance of critical intelligence or a tendency towards systematization, for artists would then be without originality. And finally, it cannot be induced by specially powerful impulses, for highly passionate or intensely energetic people are not necessarily original; it cannot be simply regarded as equivalent to intelligence, for even highly intelligent people may be quite lacking in originality; and lastly, it is not a mere consequence of a revolutionary tendency—of rejection of what is traditional—for this, if it could stand alone, would produce a merely critical and not a productive mind.

If, however, originality is a product neither of intelligence nor of the intensity of impulse or inhibition, we are obliged to seek the founts of this enigmatic characteristic in the *quality* of the latter functions. The development of the impulses themselves, the manner in which the interests are built up on them, and the points at which the inhibitions act—these are the things that must differ from the ordinary and be unusual or even unique in an original person. Hence, the question whether this original person will devote his activities to practical life, to art, or to science will depend upon these factors. The development of an original thought will, as we have seen, always demand an exceptional intelligence, but originality itself, and therefore the greatness of a thinker, will in the final result depend on the unusualness of the emotional components of his personality.

Since great strength of impulse, abnormal inhibition, outstanding critical intelligence, predominance of co-ordination, the impulse towards independence, and a high capacity for sublimation—*i.e.*, all the other marks of a philosopher—can coexist with any and every degree of originality, or exist without it, we can understand that any given amount of philosophic productivity may come from minds which have little independence—and even from such as, having nothing of their own to offer, merely repeat their masters' words.

In the same way as originality, the other characteristics mentioned above may show great variations of degree: differences in the intensity of the impulses, the inhibitions and the capacity for sublimation explain the varying range of philosophic activity, and this may be represented by mere philosophic interest, by keen, though only receptive, concern with philosophic problems, or it may attain the highest degree of productivity.

Variations in the degree of critical intelligence, in the tendency towards co-ordination, and in the impulse towards independence will lead solely to varying degrees of acumen, thoroughness and orthodoxy.

In sum—originality is due to an unusual structure of the emotional personality.

CHAPTER XXVII

THE CAUSES OF ABNORMALLY INTENSE INHIBITIONS

Highly intense impulses and inhibitions, great critical intelligence and power of sublimation, a weak projective capacity balanced by a strong trend towards co-ordination —such are the last factors which we have reached in our examination of the psychic structure of the philosophers. Must we be content to stop at this point or can we investigate the still less accessible depths from which *these phenomena, in their turn, spring? I believe this* to be possible at one point and that we may indeed find factors in cases of increased intensity of inhibition, which stand in causal connexion with these phenomena.

We have already spoken of hypersensitiveness, *i.e.*, the tendency to experience exceptionally vivid sensations of displeasure, as a possible cause of abnormally intense inhibitions. This hypersensitiveness finds its expression in the fact that even relatively trivial causes bring about very intense and therefore very far-reaching feelings of displeasure. Since, however, such trivial causes are found at almost every turn in everyday life, the hypersensitive person reacts with displeasure towards it; finding a hair in every dish of soup and a disagreeable side to every pleasure, he becomes dissatisfied with practical life as a whole.

A graphic example may be quoted: Prince Bodhisattva, who later became Buddha, was driving in the public gardens and happily watching the people in holiday attire who filled the well-watered and decorated streets when suddenly his spirit was seized with horror at the sight of a bent old man painfully making his way along with the aid of a stick. When his charioteer told him that it was the lot of all men—his own, too—to wither and fade, he lost all joy in the fair things about him, turned back at once, no longer cared to go about his affairs and fell to brooding dazedly. Making allowance for poetic exaggeration, we may say that this is the typical behaviour of a hypersensitive person: a happening which would cause only a slight sensation of displeasure to a normal person, and be easily overcome, gives rise to an intense and *lasting feeling*. With it is associated—and the story admirably brings out this psychological point—a correspondingly strong inhibition: the Prince turns back at once and loses all interest in his pursuits. In order to cheer him up, the story continues, the King induced him to take another drive, but he saw a sick man and learned that this fate, too, might be anyone's. Again he was seized with sadness and anxiety, again he drove home at once, shut himself off from others, shunned worldly pleasures, and brooded incessantly over the horrors of illness, the folly of those who when exposed to such dangers continue to lead a life of pleasure, and the possibilities of escaping from them himself. Here again we see enormous vulnerability and hypersensitiveness in the disproportionately strong dislike-reaction, and again we must admire the psychological penetration of the poet who saw that not only withdrawal from society and from worldly pleasures, *i.e.*, inhibition effects, but also deep philosophic reflexion were the results. And finally, when the Prince, on his third drive, saw a corpse and was told the meaning of death, he became breathless with terror, returned to the palace completely distracted, and from that hour neither wife nor child, companions nor State affairs could hold him; he fled the town in order to devote himself undisturbed to the thought of age, illness, and death. The hypersensitive individual is so inhibited by any aggregation of events fraught with displeasure that inability to cope with practical life and engrossment in philosophic thought are the things which result for him.

So much for poetry. Let us now turn to reality. Had the philosophers in reality such vulnerable and hypersensitive natures?

St Augustine says in his *Confessions* [1] that he supported the bitterest hardships in his greed for honours, gains, and wedlock. No pleasure gave him satisfaction and all his worldly amusements were followed by bitterness, through the mercy of God, as he puts it, who did not wish that anything should taste sweet to him, in order that he might be turned from his vain endeavours. "There were now gotten together," he says of himself and his companions, "the mouths of three beggars, sighing out their wants one to another and waiting upon thee that thou mightest give them their meat in due season." [2] Here we have the dissatisfaction with the world and the longing for God which are typical of the hypersensitive.

[1] p. 287. [2] p. 309.

Bruno, too, was easily rebuffed and disgusted by life's encounters. His own name for himself was "*il fastidito*."

Rousseau wrote that he had a tender heart and he ascribes to this all his life's misfortunes.[1] He was easily discouraged, easily rebuffed, and had a highly vulnerable sense of honour. In his youth he had, by a false accusation, given a girl the reputation of being a thief. This left upon him so deep and painful an impression that it saved him for the whole of his life from any act bordering on the criminal.[2]

Fichte suffered, even in later life, from the memory of the various tricks which as a boy he and his comrades had played on their schoolmasters.

Herbart says, clearly referring to himself: "A boy with delicate susceptibilities may suffer greatly; he may suffer in silence, and wounds may be inflicted which will still smart in manhood's years."[3]

Even as a quite young man Schopenhauer was a source of trouble to his mother owing to his unhappy disposition, his complaints about unavoidable things and his brooding countenance; she made it a condition, before inviting him to her evening parties, that he should refrain from all "lamentation about this foolish world and the sufferings of humanity." This tormenting dissatisfaction, this deep sorrow for the world and for life, were with him throughout his whole existence and they made his outlook dark with pessimism. It was only a short time before his death that he wrote: "The world is outward show: I should like to know who gains anything from being in it." And he was thinking of himself

[1] Bk. I (p. 17). [2] Bk. II (pp. 93-4). [3] Fritzsch, p. 10.

when he laid stress on the fact that as the intellect increases, so does sensibility—the power to suffer—grow immeasurably.[1]

Spencer gives a very characteristic account of his immense susceptibility to all sensations of displeasure, which " . . . may have been in part due to the trait which I inherited from my father—a great intolerance of painful feelings, either physical or moral. . . . It may have been that as a boy my peaceableness was in part due to a reluctance to enter into combats which entailed evil of this kind." [2]

Nietzsche, finally, had an extremely sensitive and susceptible disposition. " The smallest pebble is enough to overthrow me," he wrote to his sister, " because the machinery is now most highly complicated."[3] And Riehl said of him: " He felt the most intimate sympathy with the sufferings of others, even when they were of the tenderest and most hidden kind."[4] This outstanding sensitiveness also showed itself in his disillusionment with friends. " Did not my disappointment with Wagner and my parting with him endanger my life ? " he asks in one letter, " did it not take me nearly six years to recover from that sorrow ? "[5] He felt disillusioned in his friend Rée and bursts out with " I am nauseated at having to wade through such slime. I, of all people, who can only exist in an atmosphere of extreme cleanliness and sincerity. It will kill me. I suffer indescribably. My whole existence is poisoned." [6]

[1] *Welt als Wille und Vorstellung*, Vol. II, ch. 4. (Works Vol. III, p. 667.)
[2] *Autobiography*, I, p. 79. [3] Letters, II, p. 542. [4] p. 21.
[5] Letters, II, p. 480. [6] *Ibid.*, p. 533.

There are, it is true, but few thinkers in whose character we can point directly to oversensitiveness and thus be certain of identifying it as a cause of exceptionally strong inhibitions. We must, however, remember that this is a characteristic which is not very conspicuous and in consequence may easily have been overlooked by the biographers. It may, therefore, well be the case that far more of our philosophers possessed hypersensitive natures than we are able to determine to-day from the facts which have been recorded of them.

There is one remarkable fact which goes to strengthen this presumption. Hypersensitiveness, as everyday experience shows, is often found associated with physical fragility, weakness, or chronic illness. The remarkable fact is that we learn of a considerable number of the great thinkers that they were physically weak or suffered from chronic physical disease.

Bruno was pale-faced and slight of build, Bacon as a child was fragile and ailing, Hobbes was slight of frame with a delicate skin, a yellow face, and he ailed until his fortieth year. As a new-born child, Descartes was regarded by the doctors as unlikely to live, and as a boy he had an unusually delicate and weakly constitution which did not grow stronger in later life and is regarded as one of the causes of his early death when aged hardly 54. Locke had to fight all his life against a weak and unhealthy constitution which obliged him to lead a temperate and strictly regulated life. Spinoza suffered from tuberculosis for over twenty years and finally succumbed to it. Malebranche was tall and haggard, exceptionally thin and deformed by reason of a bent spine; as a child he had to be operated upon for stone and twenty years later he suffered from a severe affection of the stomach, apparently an ulcer, which made eating and drinking torture to him. Rousseau, as he said himself, "came into the world nearly dying" and little hope was felt that he would live: early in his life he developed an illness of the bladder which gave him great pain on numerous occasions and over a long period of time. Kant was from childhood extremely thin, with weak bones and still weaker muscles; he had in addition a bent spine and a pigeon chest which cramped his lungs and heart. Spencer as a child was so delicate that his parents several times gave up hope of rearing him. Hartmann from his twenties was afflicted with extremely painful articular rheumatism which he had acquired as a result of taking baths to cure an injury to the knee-cap. Nietzsche was taken ill when hardly 30 with a nervous disease which occasioned eye trouble and tormented him with severe headaches and vomiting for fifteen years.

Although most of these thinkers lived to a considerable age and some even into old age—the average life of the great philosophers is sixty-seven—this is no disproof of the weakness of their constitutions or the reality of their illnesses. Rather is it evidence that their passive mode of life, their aloofness from the struggle for existence, their avoidance of action and their concern with the inward life was the most practical and the healthiest form of existence for them—that is to say that the impulse which directed them to this kind of life was based on a sound instinct, viz., that "a certain kind of man is most *useful to himself* when he hinders his own action as much as possible."[1]

The weak constitution, liability to disease, or chronic illness of these men should now have furnished us with the physical basis for an abnormal sensibility towards feelings of displeasure, from which high intensity of inhibition is derived, which in its turn leads to philosophic activity.

Plato definitely emphasized this connexion between physical weakness and philosophic activity when he wrote: "Moreover, the bridle which curbs our friend Theages may be equally efficacious in other instances. For Theages is kept in check by ill-health, which excludes him from a public life, though in all other respects he has every inducement to desert philosophy."[2]

Hypersensitiveness, then, whether based upon a delicate physical constitution or upon the human emotional apparatus must, as we have said, inhibit all practical activities: the burnt child dreads the fire, but the hypersensitive person is so painfully burnt even by the minor frictions of daily life that he dreads practical life altogether and thus becomes a person of abnormal inhibitions and, in favourable circumstances, a philosopher. "The greatest men suffer most in life"[3] is Nietzsche's way of giving general expression to this relationship of cause and effect. Bychowski, however, writing of this particular case of the thinker, says: "The philosopher turns away from life because in its entirety it seems to him a wounded life,"[4] and Hitschmann: "Life must have brought

[1] Works, XIV, p. 37 (*Will to Power*, Bk. I, § 45).
[2] *Republic*, 496.
[3] *Werke*, XIII, p. 37.
[4] p. 150.

deception when its main content is these (philosophic) problems and thinking is preferred to acting."[1]

Our conclusion is, then, that one of the causes of highly intense inhibitions must be sought in the hypersensitiveness to feelings of displeasure to which we can point directly in the case of some of the great philosophers and which we can at least conjecture to have been present in many of the others by reason of their weak constitution or liability to sickness.

[1] p. 163.

CHAPTER XXVIII

THE CONSEQUENCES AS THEY AFFECT THE PSYCHOLOGY OF PHILOSOPHY

1. THE philosophers suffer from excessive inhibition and are in consequence only partially able to transform their impulses into action. The considerable impulse-energy which remains undischarged works itself out in philosophic thought. Therefore, philosophizing is an outlet for impulse.

These impulses, however, tend towards action: philosophic thinking is not their appropriate outlet but a makeshift, a substitute, an alternative for action, and when Richard Wagner says "if we had life we should not need art" and calls art "an admission of impotence,"[1] we should be quite justified in substituting "philosophy" for "art."

Therefore, philosophizing is the satisfaction of an impulse by means of an alternative to action.

2. In all philosophers philosophic thought comes to rest in some train of ideas; but an impulse only comes to rest when it is satisfied; therefore the production of these trains of thought must be in some way a source of satisfaction. This characteristic of philosophy as a satisfaction of impulse has been recognized with admirable

[1] Quoted from Rank, p. 684.

clear-sightedness by Müller-Freienfels.[1] His account shows us how the various emotional types, *i.e.*, groups of people in whom the prevalence of certain impulses—*e.g.*, the erotic or combative—is common ground, create the kind of philosophy which is adapted to their type, and this because that kind and no other is appropriate to the satisfaction of their impulses—" they do not want to acquire knowledge at any price but to sing their own song at any price," [2] as Nietzsche says; it would, however, be more correct to say that their song is what they regard as the profoundest knowledge and the satisfaction of their impulses the ultimate criterion of truth.

Therefore, definite philosophic conceptions represent thinking which satisfies impulses. Philosophizing is the satisfaction of impulses through thinking.

3. We have seen above that philosophy was originally an undifferentiated entity containing within itself the germs of poetry, religion and science. We now understand how such entities come into existence; the inhibited person makes use of all the available outlets for the satisfaction of his impulses and where, as in the beginnings of the history of the mind, the claims made upon scientific method and artistic value are not too high, he is likely to confuse philosophic thought and poetic fantasy with religious works. The differentiation only came about when the demand grew more exacting. Where, however, a trend towards religion expresses itself in philosophy, as in the case of Plato, St Augustine, and Fechner, or where poetic talent is considerable, as in Plato, Bruno, and Nietzsche, we find, even at a later

[1] p. 51.

[2] *Werke*, XI, p. 163.

date, religio-scientific or poetic-scientific forms, or even forms containing all three components.

Therefore, both the primitive and the more developed artistic-religio-scientific composite forms are to be explained by the common root of all three components in the inhibited man's trend towards expression.

4. The relationship between theoretical and practical philosophy is, as we have already seen, a psychological one. The inhibited person requires a stimulant before he can act or a sedative in order to bear inaction: the practical philosophies provide these. "Every philosophy, however it may have come into existence, serves definite educative ends, *e.g.*, serves to encourage or to calm, etc."[1] The inhibited person, however, requires in addition to this an outlet for the part of his impulse-energy which he is unable to transform into action: this is afforded him by philosophical thinking—theoretic philosophy. Hence the frequency with which both tendencies occur in one and the same person.

5. Why are the philosophers chiefly concerned with such extremely vital and pathematic problems? Why does the very essence of philosophy reside in preoccupation with such questions, at the same time as with general ones? God is the active man's helper and leader when his own efforts are insufficient. Need drives him to prayer. But the inhibited man's powers are never enough; he is always in need and he therefore requires God much more urgently. Consequently he will either become religious or be obliged to resist that temptation with all

[1] Nietzsche, *Werke*, XIII, § 97.

his might. Both are the case with the philosopher, and in both cases he is called upon to give his full attention to the problem of God. Men wish themselves all the more immortal when they have been denied joy and satisfaction on earth and therefore have a claim for compensation in the life to come. Who could need it more than the inhibited man who shuns the life for which he yet longs so ardently? He is the more likely to believe in an after-life in some form, or energetically to deny it—in either case to occupy himself with the problem. Men misunderstand free will as meaning freedom from compulsion and restraint and consequently claim it for their share: the inhibited man, again, has special reason for the claim and this leads, once more, to intense interest in the problem. Indeed, human behaviour, with its motives and aims and worth, is especially full of problems for one who finds it so infinitely difficult and full of failures. A further reason for his turning his attention to the observation of his own inward life is that it requires no kind of active intervention in the doings of the outside world. And finally, the inquiry into the significance of life becomes an acute one for the man to whom life has not justified itself by the satisfactions which it brings to the normal person but cannot bring to him because of his hypersensitiveness.

Thus we see how problems of life already important to the normal person assume quite exceptional importance for one with strong inhibitions and how, even apart from these, other and equally vital things which would cause little worry to the normal person appear in the light of problems. Philosophic wonder, which Plato and Aristotle held to be the beginning of all philosophy, appears here by no means as a purely intellectual emotion, but as one tinged by dissatisfaction with life, to face which the philosophers stand equipped with such mighty longings and such trivial practical abilities. And because their dissatisfaction is with human life—their own lives—their problems are predominantly the problems of human existence.

6. If we understand by idealism in the light of the theory of knowledge a denial that the physical world exists outside our own perception of it and by idealism in the light of metaphysics the assertion that the nature of the world is spiritual, it is remarkable how frequently these doctrines—which to the non-philosopher seem highly unreal—recur in the philosophic systems of the great thinkers. The phenomenon is, however, comprehensible if regarded as a consequence of the intense inhibitions and the hypersensitiveness of the philosophers. Because they were unable to assert themselves over life and the world, they sought to depreciate these things through the medium of scientific thought and to make them appear as mere phenomena of consciousness—dreams, outward appearances, delusions. For them, the only reality is their own world, the one in which they feel at home, live and rule—the world of thought, ideas, and spiritual reality. The fox said that the grapes beyond his reach were sour; the philosophers, more foxy still, persuade themselves that the grapes are not even real, are an optical illusion, a phenomena of consciousness, an appearance—certainly nothing truly and unmistakably

real and worth struggling for. Hypersensitiveness assists this tendency directly, as well as indirectly through the inhibitions to which it gives rise. Because the philosophers are totally unsatisfied with life as a result of their over-sensitiveness, their interest is withdrawn from the outside world to such an extent that it no longer makes anything more than a purely schematic impression upon them whilst the vividness and the reality of the inward aspects of existence increase in the same degree. Paulsen laid bare this root of idealism when he wrote: "As in every other case, Schopenhauer's theoretical idealism is of a practical kind; the inadequacy of things as they are leads to the creation of an idea of the perfect world. Thereby life as we live it is depreciated, made first valueless and then unreal: a world which does not deserve to exist is not the real world."[1] And Winterstein says: "All idealism is rooted in an unconscious tendency to depreciate the material outside world."[2] It is of importance to emphasize the fact that this tendency is completely unconscious in its operation, just as it is in melancholy and other psychoses in which as a result of severe inhibition and profound depression the idea also arises that the world is a dream and a delusion.

These, then, are the specific philosophic ideas which result from the general psychic structure of the great thinkers. And, indeed, it is a necessary consequence of the fact that philosophy is a satisfaction of impulses that philosophic thought cannot merely reconstruct reality as it is presented by everyday life, which fails to

[1] Quoted by Hitschmann, p. 150. [2] p. 199.

afford the philosopher an outlet for his impulses, but must re-think it to a great extent, or even deny it and set another in its stead. As katathymic thought[1]—that is, as a means for the expression of impulses which recast the psychic content—philosophy will tend to create an artificial environment, a world of make-believe built up of thoughts which possess, however, an almost hallucinatory vividness for their thinker and thus conjure up for him a reality better worth living in than the world of the average man with its hardships and sufferings.

The objection might be raised that not all philosophers are idealists, for some of them were materialists. In the first place, however, these were in a small minority and secondly, the defence of so preposterous a teaching as materialism is a proof of their reactive character, *i.e.*, these philosophers must have felt the need of painting the reality of the physical world in as effective and striking colours as possible in order to drive out a tendency to idealism. The very fact of raising the problem of the reality of the outer world is a sign of a deficient sense of reality, whether the answer is given in an idealistic or a materialistic sense. The deficient sense of reality, however, arises from intense hypersensitiveness and inhibition, which refuse to allow the interest in the outer world to develop along normal lines.

[1] Cf. Kretschmer, p. 34: "By katathymy we therefore understand the pathematic recasting of psychic content."

CHAPTER XXIX

CONCLUSION: THE PSYCHO-HYGIENIC VALUE OF PHILOSOPHY

INADEQUATE satisfaction of the impulses is a source of suffering; when it lasts for a long time it is also one of danger, since it may lead to neurosis. The danger grows with the intensity of the impulses and that of the inhibitions; the impulsive and highly inhibited person is foredoomed to nervous illness. Only an unimpeded outlet for the pent-up impulses can save him, and such an outlet is provided, not only by artistic and religious but also by philosophic pursuits. The pursuit of philosophy is thus, for those capable of it, of high psycho-hygienic value; it is for them, mentally, a form of gymnastics which is indispensable for the preservation of health and a substitute for the practical pursuits which are necessary if nervous illness is to be avoided. In so far as philosophic thinking thus acts as a safety-valve, it appears to me that this particular activity, which is often called useless and harmful, fulfils a highly important function, *i.e.*, philosophic thinking acquires a psycho-hygienic value and thus a biological utility in the preservation of the individual, for this depends to no small extent upon the maintenance of his mental health.

Mental health requires not only that the impulses

shall be exercised but also that they shall be given a certain amount of satisfaction. Those to whom life denies this minimum will be the victims of neurosis. The hypersensitive individual, whose delicate susceptibilities are cruelly hurt by every disillusionment and every pain, in whom every feeling of displeasure leaves inirradicable traces, can but be filled with the deepest dissatisfaction with the practical life which repeatedly deals him heavy blows. And whether his outward life is lived in a garret or in a palace, he always takes his ego with him and it is his own personality which will always make him suffer. No reality can satisfy him, for every reality hurts him and consequently he soon becomes afraid to face it and never learns to master it. Lack of satisfaction for his impulses will make him a victim of neurosis unless he is endowed with artistic, religious, or philosophic creative ability to conjure up for him a world which is more beautiful, more friendly and more amenable; a world which does not hurt and repel him, one in which he can live and be active—even though the activity be only thought—one that he can master and rule as king of the realm of thought. Every philosopher, Nietzsche said, represents for human life an "increase of the sense of power or the means to mask an intolerable existence."[1] Refuge in philosophy saves the person to whom it is possible from refuge in mental illness—the penultimate—and from refuge in nothingness—the ultimate—escape from the disillusionments of life. Although, it is true, neurosis or psychosis, with their accompanying states of semi-consciousness, of delirium,

[1] *Werke*, XIII, § 54.

hallucination and delusion, conceal and colour the intolerable reality, they nevertheless torment people with other symptoms and, by reason of their unsocial character deter them from seeking the company of others. Philosophy is, however, free from the first of these evils and less affected by the second. The ties of the social world are, it is true, loosened by life in the artificial environment inherent in the system, but they are not torn as in neurosis, or completely severed, as in psychosis.

In the creation of this artificial environment, this equable climate provided for the mind at a lower cost than neurosis demands, lies a second important function of philosophic thought, and one which has a high biological value because it serves to maintain mental health and, with it, individuality itself.

There is, however, a further way in which philosophic thought can provide the necessary satisfaction of vital impulses apart from the creation of a world of illusion. The great thinkers were men of strong impulses and the longing for creative activity burned furiously within them; in Zarathustra's words they lusted to fashion millenniums in their hand like wax. But the way to the act which liberates was closed. Thereupon their impulses made a detour; they created philosophic thoughts, great and world-shaking ideas, which in turn brought their creators that for which they longed, but could not find in action—the satisfying sensation of effective effort and of creation—and did not deny them even the highest degree of this sensation—the enjoyment of power and fame.[1]

[1] See Freud, pp. 435 ff., where the same ideas are developed in respect of artists.

This is the third psycho-hygienically important function of philosophic thought, viz., that it affords an alternative path for effective effort in life for those who cannot take the direct path, that of deeds. Moreover, it serves, by creating this detour, to bring about real and not merely illusory satisfaction of educational and political interests and of ambition, and thus again helps to provide the amount of satisfaction requisite to mental health.

Thus the biological value of philosophy is threefold. Philosophic thought firstly serves as a substitute for practical action in the discharge of excess impulse-energies—secondly, it creates, in the place of harsh and intractable and therefore unsatisfying reality, a painless and tractable and therefore satisfying world—and thirdly, it leads, by means of a detour, to the real satisfaction of powerful interests. And in all three ways it serves to maintain mental health: its value lies in the realm of psychic hygiene.

If philosophic activity can serve as a safety-valve for pent-up impulses, this function is by no means restricted to the thinkers of genius but must also apply to less independent minds. Nevertheless, the latter are to a great extent thrown back upon the works of the great, which furnish them with inspiration, groundwork, and an indication of direction in forming their own thoughts. And it is in this service, which, as it were, turns the great philosophers into vast reservoirs of mental power and health for numbers of people, that one of the cultural merits of their works resides.

Similarly, the satisfaction which a philosophy provides by creating an artificial environment is by no means restricted to its creators, for the same consoling and elevating effects may be shared by anyone with a nature at all resembling theirs who treads the same paths consciously and in good faith. Thus the magic garden which a powerful spirit has created to shelter it from the inclemencies of life, becomes a public pleasure-ground affording recreation and health to many of life's wounded who have no plot of earth of their own. In this a second cultural merit of the great philosophies resides.

Hence we cannot agree with Schopenhauer that the works of genius serve no useful end and that, whilst all other human work serves to support life and to ease it, it is of the essence of philosophy to be useless.[1] On the contrary, they serve in just the same way to support and ease our lives, for our lives depend to a vast extent upon the health of our minds.

[1] *Welt als Wille und Vorstellung*, Vol. II, Bk. III, ch. 31.

BIBLIOGRAPHY

AUGUSTINE, ST, *Confessions*. Latin and translated by W. WALLS. London, 1912.

BIRNBAUM, KARL, *Psychopathologische Dokumente*. 1920.

BOROWSKI, LUDWIG ERNST, *Darstellung des Lebens und Charakters Immanuel Kants*. Deutsche Bibliothek. 1912.

BRAUN, OTTO, *Eduard v. Hartmann*. Frommanns Klassiker der Philosophie. Vol. 20. 1909.

BÜHLER, KARL, *Ursprung des Intellekts*. "*Die Naturwissenschaften*." Vol. 8. 1921.

BURTON, JOHN HILL, *Life and Correspondence of David Hume*. 2 Vols. Edinburgh, 1846.

BYCHOWSKI, GUSTAV, *Metaphysik und Schizophrenie*. 1923.

CONRAD, *Grundriss der politischen Ökonomie*. Statistik 4. I. 5th Imp., 1923.

EBSTEIN, WILHELM, *Arthur Schopenhauer. Seine wirklichen und vermeintlichen Krankheiten*. 1907.

FECHTNER, EDUARD, *John Locke: ein Bild aus den geistigen Kämpfen Englands im 17 Jahrh*. Stuttgart, 1898.

FISCHER, KUNO, *Bacon und seine Nachfolger*. 2nd Imp., 1875.

— *Geschichte der neueren Philosophie*. Vol. 2. *Spinozas Leben, Werke und Lehre*. 5th Imp., 1909.

— Vol. 3. *Leibniz*. 5th Imp., 1920.

— Vol. 7. *Schelling*. 4th Imp., 1923.

— Vol. 8. *Hegel*. 2nd Imp., 1911.

FREUD, SIGMUND, *Vorlesungen zur Einführung in die Psycho-analyse*. 2nd Imp., 1918. [*Introductory Lectures on Psycho-analysis*. Translated by J. RIVIERE. London, 1922.]

FRITZSCH, T., *Herbarts Leben und Lehre*. *Natur und Geisteswelt*. Vol. 164. 1921.

GAUPP, OTTO, *Herbert Spencer*. Frommanns Klassiker der Philosophie. Vol. 5. 3rd Imp., Stuttgart, 1906.

Gebhardt, Karl, *Spinoza, Lebensbeschreibungen und Gespräche*. Philosophische Bibliothek. Vol. 96b. 1914. Meiner.

Gomperz, Heinrich, *Psychologische Beobachtungen an grieschischen Philosophen*. 1924.

Gwinner, Wilhelm v., *Schopenhauers Leben*. 3rd Imp., 1910.

Hitschmann, Eduard, *Schopenhauer*. "*Imago*," 2nd year. Vol. 2. 1913.

Hoche, A., *Zum Leib-Seele-Problem*. "*Die Naturwissenschaften*." Vol. 47. 1924.

Höffding, Harald, *Rousseau und seine Philosophie*. Frommanns Klassiker der Philosophie. 1896.

Hoffmann, Abraham, *Descartes*. Frommanns Klassiker der Philosophie. Vol. 18. 2nd Imp., 1923.

Jachmann, Reinhold Bernhard, *Immanuel Kant*. Deutsche Bibliothek. 1912.

James, William, *Principles of Psychology*. New York, 1890.

Jaspers, Karl, *Psychologie der Weltanschauungen*. 1919.

Jodl, Friedrich, *Ludwig Feuerbach*. Frommanns Klassiker der Philosophie. Vol. 17. Stuttgart, 1921.

Kant, Immanuel, *Prolegomena*. Kirchmanns philosophische Bibliothek. *Kants Werke*. Vol. III. 4th Imp., 1905. [*Prolegomena to any Future Metaphysics*. Translated by P. Carns. Chicago, 1902.]

— *Versuch über die Krankheiten des Kopfes*. Kirchmanns philosophische Bibliothek. *Kants Werke*. Vol. 8.

King, Lord, *The Life of John Locke*. London, 1829.

Kretschmer, Ernst, *Medizinische Psychologie*. 1922.

Lasswitz, Kurd, *Fechner*. Frommanns Klassiker der Philosophie. Vol. 1. 3rd Imp., 1910.

Mackay, John Henry, *Max Stirner*. 2nd Imp., 1910.

Medicus, Fritz, *Fichtes Leben*. 2nd Imp., 1922.

Mill, John Stuart, *Autobiography*. 2nd Ed. London, 1873.

Morgan, Conwy Lloyd, *Habit and Instinct*. London, 1896.

Müller-Freienfels, Richard, *Persönlichkeit und Weltanschauung*. 1919.

Nietzsche, Friedrich, *Werke*. Leipzig, 1900-13.

— *Complete Works*, edited by Dr Oscar Levy. Edinburgh and London. 1909-13.

— *Briefe an Mutter und Schwester*. 1909.

Ostwald, Wilhelm, *Auguste Comte*. 1914.

PAULSEN, FRIEDRICH, *Einleitung in die Philosophie*. 24th Imp., 1912. [*Introduction to Philosophy*. Translated by F. THILLY, 2nd Ed. New York, 1906.]

— *Immanuel Kant*. Frommanns Klassiker der Philosophie. Vol. 7. 6th Imp., 1920.

PLATO, *The Dialogues of Plato*. Translated by B. JOWETT, 2nd Ed. Oxford, 1875.

RANK, OTTO, *Das Inzest-Motiv in Dichtung und Sage*. 1912.

RIEHL, ALOYS, *Friedrich Nietzsche*. Frommanns Klassiker der Philosophie. Vol. 6. 4th Imp.

— *Giordano Bruno*. 2nd Imp., 1900.

ROUSSEAU, JEAN JACQUES, *Les Confessions*. Paris, 1913.

— *Les Confessions, suivies des Rêveries du Promeneur solitaire*. Geneva, 1782.

— *Les Confessions, 2e partie*. 1786-90.

SCHMIDT, HEINRICH, *Epikurs Philosophie der Lebensfreude*. 1921.

SCHOPENHAUER, ARTHUR, *Sämtliche Werke*. 2nd Imp. (Brockhaus), 1916.

SCHULTZ, JULIUS, *Die Philosophie am Scheidewege*. 1922.

SIEBECK, HERMANN, *Aristoteles*. Frommanns Klassiker der Philosophie. Vol. 8. 4th Imp., 1922.

SPENCER, HERBERT, *Autobiography*. London, 1904.

SPRANGER, EDUARD, *Lebensformen*. 4th Ed., Halle, 1924.

THOMSEN, ANTON, *David Hume*. Berlin, 1912. [*David Hume: Hans Liv og hans Filosofi*. Copenhagen, 1911.]

TÖNNIES, FERDINAND, *Thomas Hobbes*. Frommanns Klassiker der Philosophie. Vol. 2. 2nd Imp.

UEBERWEG, FRIEDRICH, *Berkeley, Prinzipien der menschlichen Erkenntnis*. 4th Imp., 1917.

WILAMOWITZ-MOELLENDORF, ULRICH v., *Platon*. 1919.

WINDELBAND, WILHELM, *Platon*. Frommanns Klassiker der Philosophie. Vol. 9. 1900.

WINTERSTEIN. ALFRED v., *Psychoanalytische Anmerkungen zur Geschichte der Philosophie*. "*Imago*," 2nd year. Vol. 2. 1913.

INDEX OF NAMES

INDEX OF NAMES

PRINTED IN GREAT BRITAIN BY
THE EDINBURGH PRESS, 9 AND 11 YOUNG STREET, EDINBURGH